Musa Okwonga has practised both law and football, with the emphasis on the latter. He won the Junior Bridport Prize for fiction in 1994, for poetry in 1995, and the WH Smith Young Writers competition a year later. His first book, *A Cultured Left Foot*, was longlisted for the 2008 William Hill Sports Book of the Year Award. He lives in East London.

WILL YOU MANAGE?

The necessary skills to be a great gaffer

Musa Okwonga

A complete catalogue record for this book can be obtained from
the British Library on request

First published in 2010 by Serpent's Tail,
an imprint of Profile Books Ltd
3A Exmouth House
Pine Street
London EC1R 0JH
website: www.serpentstail.com

ISBN 978 1 84668 724 2

Designed and typeset by sue@lambledesign.demon.co.uk
Printed by Clays, Bungay, Suffolk

10 9 8 7 6 5 4 3 2 1

CONTENTS

ACKNOWLEDGEMENTS

Without the time, guidance and inspiration of the following people, I could not have written this book:

Vic Akers, Duncan Alexander, Guillem Balague, George Borg, Dr Sue Bridgewater, Terry Brown, George Carney, Greg Demetriou, Dr Dorian Dugmore, Mark Ellingham, John Faulkner, George Foulkes, Professor Bill Gerrard, Henry Gregg, Brent Hills, Miles Jacobson, Barry McNeill, Kirti Mandir, Gabriele Marcotti, Professor Ron Maughan, Wilson Okwonga, Raí Oliveira, Paul Simpson, Graham Turner, Andrew Wainstein, Jim White, John Williams and Gianfranco Zola.

I would like to thank my editor Pete Ayrton at Serpent's Tail; my agent Heather Holden-Brown and Elly James at HHB Agency; and Gianluca Vialli, for going the extra mile.

For Kim-Leng Hills, the Carney family, and my father

INTRODUCTION

Will you manage?

Seriously, if you stepped down there, right now, would you be able to do it better?

How hard can it be? you're asking yourself. Go on, admit it. You think you're smarter. You think you could do a better job than he has. You're staring at that supposedly world-class manager sitting on that bench. Then you're staring in disbelief at the team that he's selected. Then you're staring back at him, your disbelief increasing all the while. How is it – who is he – that he's been given the chance to get these tactics so wrong?

The worst thing is that he doesn't even *look* that special. There's nothing about his appearance which reassures you that he's on a higher intellectual plane than you, that makes you think, "Actually, you know, he's a genius. He's an Einstein sort of fellow." There's no wild streak of silver in his hair that marks him out as a maverick in the style of, say, the boxing promoter Don King; his posture as he watches the game unfold before him is far from imperial.

In fact, he's stern and stiff. His shoulders are hunched so far inward that it's as if they're trying to headbutt each other, whilst his shoulder blades are jutting almost visible stab wounds out of the back of his puffer jacket. When he stands and wanders about, he doesn't look like a sergeant marshalling his troops about the pitch. Nor does he look professorial, as is so often claimed. He looks like – like – like a commuter. Like that guy who's standing in front of you in the queue at a quarter to nine at the coffee place just outside your office. Like the guy on the other side of the street, who may or may not beat you to the taxi that you've both just flagged on that long, cold, wet night. You're thinking: *he doesn't look like all that. I'm smarter than he is.*

Or, at least, that's what I was thinking; that I was smarter than him. It was 15 November 2008, and he was Arsène Wenger. He was the manager of a club whose first eleven had just defeated Manchester United, the reigning English and European champions, by two goals to one in one of the finest matches in recent years; manager of a club whose second eleven, with an average age of around twenty, had decimated full-strength Premier League and Championship opposition in the last two rounds of the Carling Cup, firing nine goals without reply. What's more, on his way to one of three English league titles, he'd led his team undefeated through an entire campaign; his Invincibles, as they became known, won twenty-six and drew twelve of their thirty-eight matches in the 2003–04 season.

But that was three Frenchmen and a stadium ago: Thierry Henry, Robert Pirès and Patrick Vieira had moved on from Arsenal, and Arsenal had moved on from Highbury. Four years later, during as half-hearted an autumn as the Met Office can remember, I was sitting on high in the Emirates stadium, directly above Wenger, as if in judgement on his efforts. There was a storm somewhere up in those off-colour clouds that couldn't decide whether to break loose; and neither could Arsenal. With the exception of Theo Walcott, whose every sprint summoned excitement in the hearts of the most apathetic of corporate guests, there was no one else in the team who looked like troubling the speed cameras.

Now, it wasn't like Arsenal weren't quick: Bacary Sagna and Gael Clichy were as rapid a pair of full-backs as you could find anywhere. It's just that there was an alarming lifelessness about their play; and, though Wenger didn't know why it was going wrong, I knew all too well.

Who was I? Well, I was managing a team of my own. Whilst Wenger's Arsenal was fourth in their Premier League, I was faring somewhat worse in mine; in the FA's fantasy football version of the top division, as the coach of "Frail Madrid", I was down in 253,585th place, out of a total of 1,726,943 players. However, I'd experienced extraordinary success in another format of this game. During one season of the football game *Championship Manager*, I took charge of Parma and I defeated Real Madrid 8–0 in the UEFA Cup. Away from home. Yes, that's right, eight goals *plus* a clean sheet; and I did it in the valley of the shadow of the Santiago Bernabéu itself, where many a proud defensive record has met a grisly end.

And what did I know that Wenger didn't as I sat above him, my sense of smugness wrapped around me as tightly as my cardigan? Well, I knew that he should have brought off Nicklas Bendtner, what, fourteen, fifteen, sixteen minutes ago?... – Seventeen. – Eighteen. I knew that Samir Nasri was not the new Robert Pirès. Yes, he scored vital goals, as had his fellow Gaul; recently, and painfully, he'd scored twice against my team, Manchester United, in that aforementioned 2–1 victory. But he was too small, you see; when he wasn't scoring goals, he wasn't a sufficiently physical factor to justify his position as a starter for Arsenal. And there was Denilson next to him, the stiletto-thin Brazilian, who looked equally bewildered... And Bendtner was still on the pitch; *still*; Wenger should have brought him off, what, nineteen, twenty minutes ago...

If you're as sure in your football opinions as I was when judging Wenger, then the chances are that you've got the essence of a great manager in you. An element of greatness in this job, after all, is the guts to stand firm in the face of opposing views from players, coaching staff, fans on post-match phone-ins; and Wenger, having spent some years coaching in Japan, was possessed that evening of an appropriately Zen-like concentration. As he would tell the *Daily Telegraph* some weeks later, "When you are focused you sometimes don't even notice the rain."

Of course, there's more to greatness than being superbly stubborn; there are several other gifts you'll need in order to amount to a Marcello Lippi, a Jock Stein, or a Rinus Michels. So many more, in fact, that we'll look at many areas in which successful bosses must excel. Should you wish to emulate them, you must not only have a clear and compelling vision for each club that you join; you must also, through fine man management, be able to carry it out. You'll need to be abreast of the latest training techniques, and to have the last word in tactical innovation. All the while, you should be well versed in – or, at least, well aware of – the machinations of club politics, so that you'll be able to negotiate the dense web of egos and vested interests that manifest themselves at boardroom level. Finally, fundamentally, you should be able to handle the media with consummate confidence.

We'll get to those matters later. For now, though, we should ask ourselves how we've come to this place, where we dare so regularly and so ruthlessly to question the methods of these exalted managers: and we should ask ourselves whether we're at all responsible, because they're becoming more and more of an endangered species with every passing season. Research conducted by Dr Sue Bridgewater at the University of Warwick has shown that, in the Football League, the average tenure of a manager was 2.7 years in 1992; by 2005, it had dropped to 1.7 years. By any measure, that's an eye-catching decline; and an American writer has come as close as anyone to explaining it.

• 5 •

In *The Tipping Point* Malcolm Gladwell, the social scientist and best-selling author, argues that "ideas and products and messages and behaviors spread just like viruses do". Further, he notes that there are three characteristics that enable such a spread. As Gladwell explains: "These three characteristics – one, contagiousness; two, the fact that little causes can have big effects; and three, that change happens not gradually but at one dramatic moment – are the same three principles that define how measles moves through a grade-school classroom or the flu attacks every winter. Of the three, the third trait – the idea that epidemics can rise or fall in one dramatic movement – is the most important... The name given to that one dramatic moment in an epidemic when everything can change all at once is the Tipping Point... the Tipping Point is the moment of critical mass, the threshold, the boiling point."

There was a tipping point in the early nineties, after which football managers came under more scrutiny than ever before. At this moment, there was a perfect storm, where three powerful fronts came together. There was Sky's acquisition of a multi-year monopoly over Premiership TV rights; there was the arrival of the computer game, *Championship Manager*; and there was *Fantasy Football League*, the programme that took football analysis fully mainstream.

The impact of Sky TV was to create, in the form of programmes such as *Soccer Saturday*, twenty-four hour coverage of football. Every last transfer rumour and tactical switch was analysed to the point of tedium, and then far beyond; there could now be no respite for the beleaguered boss. Within a couple of years *Championship Manager*, the virtual football management game, established itself as a recreation of Class A addictiveness.

And then there were Frank Skinner and David Baddiel who came from an unacknowledged netherworld between two types of man. Before these two comedians co-hosted

Fantasy Football League, an irreverent and hilarious look at the professional game, male football fans had only really come in two types; publicly, at least. There was the geezer – the boozy, laddish type who only ever seemed to roam around town with clones of himself. And then there was the geek.

The geek felt it his mortal duty to stash in his memory any stat ever produced by the beautiful game. The geek was in a difficult position when he hung out in the vicinity of geezers. He was smarter than they were and could talk them under the table when it came to tactical chat, but he wasn't as cool. Meanwhile, the geezers felt similarly awkward. Here was this smart-aleck whom they could comfortably drink under the table, but – though hugely irritating to be around – actually had expertise that they greatly envied. And so this uncomfortable state of affairs continued until Skinner and Baddiel came along, who were half-geezer, half-geek.

For the first time, you had two world-class comedians whose sole brief was to lacerate the football world, week in, week out. Gladwell has written – contentiously, it must be noted – that "social epidemics [are] driven by the efforts of a handful of exceptional people", and that's what, in this instance, Skinner and Baddiel were: the former had a Masters degree from Warwick University, and the latter had a double-first from Cambridge. Within football, it was now officially cool to wield your intelligence as proudly as your sixth pint of Guinness.

Fans were now liberated to infuse even the most drunken pub conversations with a fresh and scholarly nuance. Socrates the philosopher was referred to as readily as Socrates the player. Football men have never been the quickest to laugh at themselves, and early on several noses were put memorably, if cruelly, out of joint. In response, Sheffield United's Dave Bassett referred to Baddiel and Skinner darkly, if accurately, as "comedians". Ian St John, who had previously hosted a hit show of his own with Jimmy Greaves, commented that "all they were doing was taking the piss. Anyone could do that. They had no ideas."

St John's criticism was unfair: the "Phoenix from the Flames" segment of the show, in which Skinner and Baddiel recreated great goals of the past with the aid of the original players – now retired, and a very long way from fitness – was genius. But that's moot. Thanks to Sky, *Championship Manager* and *Fantasy Football League*, you could now endlessly watch, coach and mock your favourite players; and you could forever second-guess the decisions that their managers made. Losing 2–0 to Villa? You'd never have done that. Why, just last night you were playing Villa on your PC, and you thrashed them 4–0 with your reserve side. And so on, and so forth. All of a sudden we weren't criticising football managers from the comfort of our armchairs, which we'd always done before; now, we were actually on the bench with them.

What was all of this doing to managers? Not much good, as it turned out. I spoke with Dr Dorian Dugmore, at the Adidas Wellness Centre; Dr Dugmore and his team currently work with 120 current or former Football League managers, including "all but three or four" of the Premier League bosses. At the Centre, they offer "an holistic service, 'Fit to Manage'," which assesses each patient for heart, cancer and other lifestyle risks. Dr Dugmore compared the lot of a football manager to that of any eminent corporate figure, noting crucially that "the big difference, really, is very often media attention. Chief executives of big companies, of which we have many on the programme, have similar stresses and pressures, but what they don't have is the massive media attention on everything that they do. You open the paper in the morning, it's there; you walk out the front door, and the cameras are snapping. It's there all the time."

The average working week of a Premier League football

manager was "easily" 80 to 100 hours, and often more, said Dr Dugmore. "The average Premiership manager," he related, "can easily work that, looking at players, looking at other teams' performances… they'll eat fast food out of motorway cafes, they'll skip meals, they'll go to bed late… the body has to sleep. It needs time to repair, to recuperate. And if you're constantly changing the demands you're making on the body, and on the heart particularly, then eventually there's a price to pay for that." What kind of price, I wondered?

"We've heart-tested 120 managers," he replied, "and between 40 and 50 per cent of them have cardiovascular risk factors that need to be addressed." If not, they were likely to end up like Johan Cruyff, Graeme Souness and Gérard Houllier, who had heart operations involving a good few bypasses between them. Following this bracing conversation, I contacted Dr Sue Bridgewater, who in addition to her research also directed the Certificate for Applied Management in Football, a course whose alumni included Mark Hughes, Stuart Pearce, and Paul Ince. She sounded equally concerned about this predicament.

"What does always strike me is the human cost," she remarked. "I remember one of the Premier League managers saying to me, 'When we win, I feel relieved. Normally, on match day morning, I feel sick.' And you think of that pressure they're putting themselves under. You can get on the pitch and kick a ball when you're a player, but as a manager once [the players] cross the line there's not a lot you can do, and you know you're going to be held accountable."

"When you see them go through what they go through," she continued, "I don't see why anyone would want to be a football manager… Part of my introduction now [to the course] is to say, 'This is a huge step. Look at this. Be aware that if you go into this, you're going to be sacked, it's going to be painful, and ask yourself a question: Do you want to do this? If so, fine, we'll help you as much as we can.'" I was speaking to Dr Bridgewater on the telephone, but I could almost hear her shrugging at the end of the line. Why, to her apparent exasperation, were football managers drawn to the profession like lemmings to the brink of a cliff? Why did they seek out careers in which most were doomed to fail?

But, in playing the catcher in the rye, Dr Bridgewater was asking the wrong questions. As the old saying goes, "Man cannot reason himself out of that which he did not reason himself into." There's a very large group of people who don't understand why people are obsessed with football; there's an even larger group of people, like the respected academics and physicians above, who don't understand why anyone would want to manage a football team, real or virtual. Both of those groups include managers themselves. They recognise it as both a calling and a compulsion, a profession with which, whether or not it rewards them, they must make peace.

After all, being a manager is partly about preparing yourself for a lifetime of being second best; of suiting up for a drama in which you're more likely than not to end up as the punchline. The thought of those managers lining up only to be knocked down has something of a tragic romanticism about it; and since no one has ever really done tragedy like the ancient Greeks, it's probably best to turn to them.

"Greek tragedy" is a phrase that's often used in connection with sport, but too rarely dissected; it's like one of those slightly curveball expressions that someone throws into casual conversation, like *esoteric* or *quixotic*, and in order to keep up with the intellectual Joneses you nod politely as if you know what they're talking about. But in reality you're not quite sure. I always thought that, in sport, the prime example of Greek tragedy was where someone – like, say, the disgraced Canadian sprinter Ben Johnson – was undone by a flaw in their character, a little like Icarus getting cocky and flying too close to the sun with his wax wings.

But that's not totally correct; there's a subtle difference. The true Greek tragedy, says Aristotle in his *Poetics*, is a situation where an imperfect but essentially decent guy makes a terrible but understandable mistake, or *hamartia*; an honest mistake, not one linked to the deepest fault lines in his ego, but a simple and spectacular miscalculation. As Aristotle writes, the misfortune would typically befall "the sort of person who is not outstanding in moral excellence or justice; on the other hand, the change to bad fortune which he undergoes is not due to any moral defect or depravity, but to an error of some kind."

A Greek tragedy, on this analysis, was Kevin Keegan's *hamartia* to return as Newcastle United's manager in January 2008. In fact, so Greek was Keegan's return that it made me think of Dr Spence.

Dr Spence was my GCSE history teacher, and we had a big disagreement once, which was mainly to do with the fact that he was brilliant and correct, and that I was conceited and wrong. It was nothing vocal; nothing heated; I doubt he even remembers it. It was to do with an essay that I wrote about World War I, in which I argued that, after a certain point, the outbreak of that conflict was inevitable. When I received the essay back, I saw a few short, red slashes through the word "inevitable", and Dr Spence's explanatory comment that "Nothing is inevitable in history. At most, things are only increasingly probable."

Well, I didn't have his phone number to hand and I hadn't seen him in years, but I would gladly have told Dr Spence that Kevin Keegan's acrimonious departure from St James' Park was as inevitable as it gets: as inevitable as an England batting collapse in the mid-1980s, inevitable as the Rolling Stones doing *just* one more tour. So mercurial and impulsive had Keegan been in his managing career, suddenly walking away from the England job in 2000 because he felt that he couldn't do it justice, that you expected something incendiary to happen. The best summary of Keegan's appointment came, via email, from a friend of mine:

> Isn't it great though? Football should be entertaining... I'm a relatively chaste individual. I am normally sober, I don't take drugs, I stay faithful to the missus. I will take my footballing pleasures where and how I will. This is the footballing equivalent of a carefree quickie with an old flame...it's probably not the best idea in the world and it likely won't last forever, but it keeps the heart pumping and keeps out the cold for a while.

Keegan departed, in duly acrimonious fashion, only eight months later (but, it must be said, with his dignity perfectly intact). In many ways, football managers such as Keegan have become our fall guys; and in the midst of all this it's important for managers, and their advocates, to restate the difficulty of what it is they do. Great management, after all, is an act of craftsmanship, a mastery of many disparate trades. In a 2007 interview with *The Times*, the then Derby manager Paul Jewell quoted a mentor of his who had advised him that "to be a manager, you've got to be a boss, a friend, a money lender, a marriage guidance counsellor – the only thing you haven't got to be is a gynaecologist. But then again, you're dealing with c**ts every day!"

Jewell (to tabloid delight, inevitably) would eventually fall upon hard marital times of his own, but his point still holds true. A strong shout in favour of the *Championship Manager* (now known as *Football Manager*) series of games is that they have shown millions of players the exceptional complexity of managerial life – and the attendant neuroses that it produces. The buying, the selling, the fact that you've got to massage the egos of thirty squad players at the same time even though you've only got one pair of hands; the tactics, the contract tussles… it's a discipline that demands total immersion, and which all too regularly gets it. I can confess that, whilst at law school, I played an edition of this game so intensely that it gave me a severe warning – at the end of one particularly long session, it advised me in you-naughty-boy italics to *Remember that there is an outside world.*

Football management is a profession of often overwhelming loneliness. Sir Alex Ferguson, not typically regarded as the most sensitive of souls, has commented that "as a manager there are a lot of moments in every week when you feel very much on your own. People don't want to knock on your door because they think you're busy all the time when the truth is you can be sitting there twiddling your thumbs. You can fill your time by phoning other managers but there are a lot of hours spent on your own."

Let's be grateful, then, to *Football Manager*; because it allows us, to some degree, to empathise with the greats. All those hours of joyous isolation spent craned over a PC give us a taste of the real thing; the mounting euphoria as you plot your way through each round of the cup, or the gathering dread as you spiral, slowly and surely as a sycamore seed, down the league table; and then you save the game, turn that computer off, and you're sitting there with no one; and by now, it'll be so late that the whole world is still, and you'll lie there with dry eyes, dry throat and the echo of an empty gut, so consumed by that cruel injury to your number 10 or that last-minute equaliser away at Roma that you've forgotten to feed or water yourself for endless hours.

And then you're there, knowing what it feels like to manage. Having sunk yourself into the onrushing thrill of it all, you've now thrust your head back out above the crashing surf, and seen that everyone's sailed on without you. There'll be the missed calls, the cancelled dates, the cold dinners. And, sooner or later, you'll sink yourself back in.

As I'd looked down there at Wenger, he'd clearly sunk himself back in; he was in a strange kind of solitude, sixty thousand people watching as he tied himself up in his thoughts. For his own sake, you hoped that he wasn't feeling too adrift. John Caccioppo and William Patrick, in their book *Loneliness: Human Nature and the Need for Social Connection*, note that "Social isolation has an impact on health comparable to the effect of high blood pressure, lack of exercise, obesity, or smoking." They continue: "To measure a person's level of loneliness, researchers use a psychological assessment tool called the UCLA Loneliness Scale, a list of twenty questions with no right or wrong answers."

I wondered if, in their darker moments, football managers might ever consider taking the UCLA test. It's pretty short and simple; the kind of thing that they can easily complete on the coach ride home from that 5–0 annihilation at Chelsea, or the morning after that televised press conference in which they ranted about everything from the Cup draw to the breakdown of the family unit. The UCLA test includes faintly ominous enquiries, such as "How often do you feel that your interests and ideas are not shared by those around you?", and "How often do you feel that people are around you but not with you?" The maximum that you can score on the test is 80; the threshold for "high loneliness" is 44; and as Gabriel Agbonlahor surged through a centre-back's cotton-wool challenge to drive in Villa's second, you could sense Wenger's total rising steadily towards 70.

Why then, Arsène, and those like you? Why, in the face of hard facts and harsher fans, warned by a scornful chorus of physicians, psychologists and philosophers, did you do it? Why did you manage?

Simple. For the thrill of conducting your eleven-man orchestra in some of the most glorious fields and festival halls known to football, from Hackney Marshes to Anfield to Boca

Juniors' La Bombonera, and beyond. For the chance to watch your side, *your side*, flow endlessly from one end of the pitch to the other; or, almost tearfully, to see your back four, faced by a fleet of vengeful forwards, standing eternally firm as Stonehenge.

Part pastime, part obsession, football management's a special and bizarre business; and so our examination of it will take us to some necessarily special and bizarre places. We'll look at the threat that golf poses to football, and the advice that José Mourinho apparently took from a Chinese management consultant; we'll relive what's probably the greatest team-talk in the world; we'll even talk of princes and pendulums.

But for now, in as good a place to begin as any, we'll start with a craving.

OBSESSION

Football.

It's with you whilst you sleep, but it truly claims you as soon as you wake. Then it's upon you, even as you take your first peek at the ceiling and then snap your eyelids shut in grim denial of the day, even as you or your partner peels away the duvet and lets all that carefully-gathered warmth out into the cruel clutches of the morning.

Football! Where can you see it first? Now you're clambering for it, across piles of clothes, or across the unlucky limbs of your now-scowling partner, stretching for your phone so you can scour the Internet for last night's scores – you scour, you don't search, and you sure as hell don't surf, those verbs are too casual for an action as passionate as this – or you're barely dressed and in front of your TV, tapping frantically away at the remote control to summon Teletext; or you're gripping a newspaper, whose back page, for you, is always its front page. Never mind where North Korea has just tested its next nuke; never mind which big bank has just folded or been sold; that can all wait. What matters now is what Wayne Rooney or Leo Messi or Steven Gerrard did in the 75th minute last night.

The thing is, you already know what happened. You were in the pub, leaping into the arms of similarly worshipful punters, or banging your fist on your dashboard as the joyful announcement of their goals soared forth from the radio.

But you have to read the news and find out again. You see, if you're obsessed with football, then it's like the sun, your next pay cheque, or the front door of your parents' home: you always judge where you are in relation to it. Because football is in you, not in your veins – that's too shallow; it's in your bone marrow.

The wandering manager

As a manager, it's a requirement that you can't get enough of the game; nothing other than lifelong devotion will do, and there are those who will get their fix wherever they can. Dettmar Cramer, who managed Bayern Munich to European Cup success in 1975 and 1976, had a career whose fervour and scope matched that of a missionary; he went anywhere in the world in pursuit of football, taking jobs in – among other places – the USA, Japan, Malaysia and Saudi Arabia. And then there's Bora Milutinović, the itinerant Serb, who remains the only man to have coached five countries at the World Cup finals; between 1986 and 2002, he was in charge of Mexico, Costa Rica, the USA, Nigeria and China. Finally, and maybe most impressively, there's Giovanni Trappatoni and Ernst Happel, who are the only men to have managed their teams to league championships in four different countries: Trappatoni in Austria, Italy, Germany and Portugal; and Happel in Germany, Holland, Belgium and his native Austria.

To travel far and wide as a manager is one thing; to succeed is quite another. The Dutchman Guus Hiddink has been as effective at assimilating as anyone in the game, with a resumé of compelling breadth. Holland, Australia, Russia and South Korea are even more dissimilar in culture than they are in footballing philosophy, yet Hiddink took them all to major tournaments, where they performed either to or beyond expectations. There are two particular highlights; Australia lost by a single, highly controversial, last-minute penalty in the second round of the 2006 World Cup to Italy, the eventual winners; and South Korea, whom he coached as the host nation at the 2002 World Cup, finished fourth in the tournament, following victories over Portugal, Italy and Spain.

Some would say that what Hiddink achieved with South Korea was worthy of a knighthood; the grateful Asians went one step further and gave him honorary citizenship of the city of Seoul. That was only right, since they hadn't made it easy for him at first. He'd had to contend with the low expectations of the press and the public, who both took a dim view – realistically, it must be said – of their nation's prospects in the upcoming tournament. It must also be said that Hiddink didn't exactly help in building morale in the country since he'd been in charge of the Holland team that had humiliated South Korea 5–0 in the 1998 World Cup.

To some extent, therefore, the Dutchman was on a mission of atonement – although he didn't help matters by openly wandering about town with his girlfriend; an unmarried man flaunting his relationship was continually frowned and remarked upon in the socially conservative country that he'd adopted. Yet Hiddink didn't care. After all, stubbornness is the sibling of obsession, and by the time of his departure he'd transferred his single-mindedness to his players.

Obsession is important not only because it underpins a team's winning mentality, but because it's the one area in which football fans feel closest to their managers. When all's said and done, we can't honestly say that we're smarter than Arsène Wenger, but perhaps we'd like to think that we're just as crazy about the game as he is. The development of the football management game has been the best barometer for this passion of ours; and so I went to speak with one of its most successful devotees.

Fantasy Football 1: the champion

I had seen Henry Gregg only once or twice since university, so an interview with him was a welcome excuse to catch up. He'd studied politics, philosophy and economics as an undergraduate, and so his choice of profession was a logical step; he was now a lobbyist for the National Housing Federation, which urged the government to address the shortage of affordable homes in the UK. Vital as that work was, it wasn't why I'd contacted him. By day, he was an advocate for his fellow citizens; and by night, he'd proven himself a brilliant online football manager, having won the national Fantasy league.com competition in 2006.

Gregg's triumph had come after many hours spent in the company of *Championship Manager* – so many hours, in fact, that I briefly wondered whether they had affected his final class of degree. "When I was a student, I used to do all-night sessions quite regularly," he explained. "I remember going to my parents' place; they've got a shed down at the bottom of their garden; I'd go down to the shed and leave at about five o'clock in the morning." It was there, doubtless fuelled by heart-hammering amounts of caffeine, that he learned of his talent as a gaffer in the virtual world. "I won the Champions League three years in a row with Cardiff [City]," he said proudly. Buoyed by this taste of the big time, he'd tried his hand at competing against a group of his friends on Fantasyleague.com. "A friend of mine set up a league and there were just ten of us, and I think that helped me because my initial aim was just to beat the other nine players," said Gregg, "but I ended up beating the other 60,000 people who were playing it across the country." He'd taken home a cheque for £4,000, but his victory had cost him a certain amount of camaraderie. "I tried to do Fantasy League again the year after I won it," he lamented, "but everyone was so demoralised that I hadn't just won their league but the whole league across the country, that they refused to enter a league with me."

It's no surprise that Gregg's friends were somewhat demoralised. The UK has various fantasy leagues – several newspapers, including the *Sun*, *Telegraph*, *Daily Mail* and *The Times* run them for their readers – and each of them is closely fought, with only a few dozen points separating hundreds, if not thousands of contestants. This phenomenon, described by Gregg as "crack for football fans", had long since claimed me as a victim. During one year at law school, I was in the habit of returning home after a night out, sometimes at 1 a.m. or 2 a.m., and then playing *Championship Manager* until sunrise. One of the game's renowned features was its "addictiveness rating", a short sentence which reminded you each time you logged on or off how hooked you were. I knew that things had gone beyond my control when my PC advised me about the outside world.

Fantasy Football 2: the founders

Who was responsible for my fate, and that of many others like me? Andrew Wainstein, an Arsenal supporter who'd created the original *Fantasy League* in 1991, has a lot to answer for: he's indirectly caused or deepened the football addiction of millions of people worldwide. *Fantasy Football League*, a television programme based upon a version of Wainstein's game, was a great success: online incarnations soon followed, such as the aforementioned *Championship Manager* and *Football Manager*, which soon found their way into millions of homes and offices. ComScore, an American company that analyses digital data, reported that "the proportion of time being spent on these sites during office hours is significant. On the Friday before the start of the Premiership season alone, over 230,000 hours were spent on the fantasy football sites analyzed in this study [of which there were 8], and 52 per cent of them occurred during office hours."

Elsewhere, the social fallout was equally dramatic. *Football Manager* was reportedly cited in 35 UK divorce cases as a key reason why the marriage couldn't continue. What's more, the ubiquity of fantasy football led to a pretty bizarre pass where life began to imitate art. As Nick Pettigrew wrote in a November 2008 issue of *ShortList*, the free weekly magazine:

> One professional recently visited [the offices of *Football Manager*'s designers, Sports Interactive], upset that he was given 12/20 for shooting ability 'when I'm clearly at least 14/20'. It indicated how popular the game is among the footballing elite when one Premier League footballer admitted that, after training, most of his colleagues either go shopping, play golf or go home to switch on *Football Manager*.

So there was Andrew Wainstein, one of the leading minds behind a phenomenon that has wrecked homes and wasted office hours. Considering the widespread damage that he's done to society, he seemed pretty at ease with himself. Initially, he'd organised a few leagues among friends, but had then broadened that initial market to acquaintances and beyond. Soon, he began running the game by telephone, and it had quickly assumed its own momentum.

"It was long before the Web, so people would actually phone and fax in their substitutions," recalled Wainstein. "We just had a bank of people picking up the phone saying, 'Groves out', or 'Merson in'. We must have done, I don't know, five, ten thousand substitutions in a day." Some of these came from prominent footballers who, even when they weren't on the pitch, couldn't stay away from the game. "I remember Kieron Dyer, who I'm pretty sure at that stage was at Ipswich, had a Fantasy Football team," said Wainstein. "So he was one of our early subscribers... him and his mates played, and I think he was one of these people who would be on the phone on a Friday afternoon, saying, 'I want to make a substitution'."

Miles Jacobson, the managing director of Sports Interactive, had similar stories to tell me. He had been brought on board by the Collyer brothers, Paul and Oliver, who had developed *Championship Manager*. Following its name change to *Football Manager*, he presided over the game's international conquest from his office in Old Street, east London. "We sell about a million games a year globally, and there are around 3–3.5 million people playing the game a year," he said, when I'd asked him to tot up their figures. He'd noticed the true extent of his product's impact when he'd been introduced to four international players, three of whom represented England; and when they'd found out what he did for a living, they'd spent the rest of the afternoon asking him for tips on who they should buy for their fantasy teams.

Jacobson, a fervent Watford fan, seemed particularly immersed in the game when I went to speak with him. "I was playing the game last night, against Rafa Benítez – who's now manager of Manchester City in 2023. Before the match, Rafa Benítez said, 'I have full respect for Miles, we have a good relationship,' and at the end of the game – they beat us 1–0 – he said, 'They shouldn't be too disheartened by their performance'... So I get on pretty well with him. But there are other managers who are people that I don't like in real life, who I will get emotional about – I let my emotions ride over during the game, and I will say stupid things, and it ends up pissing off my players."

But, you might think, you don't really have a relationship with Rafa Benítez; and it's not 2023. And you'd be right – and wrong: you could spend so much time in front of that keyboard, obsessed with your closest rival's latest result and the injury to his centre-forward's ankle that you'd soon find yourself far adrift of reality. The average time spent playing the latest edition of *Football Manager*, revealed Jacobson, was 140 hours; almost six full days. No wonder his favourite addictiveness rating, as he told me, was "Don't forget to change your pants".

Micro-management

Historically, managers in the real world have been no less fixated with their players than their virtual counterparts. In *Calcio: A History of Italian Football*, John Foot noted that AC Milan's Nereo Rocco "was obsessive about the private lives of his players, following them in his car and checking up on their relationships. Gigi Meroni had to pretend that his girlfriend was his sister when Rocco was his manager at Torino." In the modern era, where footballers are multi-million pound assets, it's almost logical that there should be this attitude of micro-management, this observation of what your players are doing at all times.

Players themselves are keenly aware of their place under the microscope, which has made many of them predictably wary. I found this when I went to speak to Ron Maughan, the Professor of Sport and Exercise Nutrition at Loughborough University. He worked with several of the world's leading clubs, and frequently ran tests on their footballers; the routine that he described made them sound more like commodities than anything else. "When we measured all of these things on these players," said Maughan, "we'd weigh them before and after their training session; we'd weigh their drinks bottles before and after training, if they went for a pee, we collected it and weighed it; we stuck patches on their skin, and collected sweat, and we took it away and analysed it; and then we gave each of them a feedback sheet, and on the feedback sheet we had bits of charts in various colours, and we tried to make it very simple so you could very easily see, you know: Are you sweating a lot, are you somebody who's drinking enough?"

"The response from the players was astonishing," continued Maughan. "They're a desperately difficult group to reach, because every day they meet somebody trying to sell them something. Somebody wants a piece of them. But, almost without exception, we got an incredible response; and I remember somebody saying, 'Thank God you're treating us as individuals.'" Given that managers are now striving more than ever for any kind of competitive advantage, I asked him whether he thought there'd been an explosion of interest in the field of nutrition over the last few years. "It comes and goes," he said. "You might say that there's been an explosion of interest in the last few years, but, if you speak to someone like Trevor Lee at Manchester United, he's been the club dietician there for almost twenty years; so it's not as new as all that."

There was a section in Xavier Rivoire's biography of Arsène Wenger that I thought best showed the Frenchman's obsession with nutritional detail, and so I mentioned it to Professor Maughan. During his time in Japan, as the manager of Nagoya Grampus Eight, Wenger had kept a close eye on the body fat percentage of his players, sanctioning them if they failed to comply with his strictures. Masaru Hirayama, one of his players at the time, recalled, "Before each session, we were weighed and our fat was measured. We received a warning if this ratio grew to 11 or 12 per cent. And if our fat ratio exceeded that limit, we were excluded from the squad until we had worked off the excess weight."

"I think most clubs do that," said Professor Maughan. "Unfortunately, it's one thing to make the measurements; it's another thing to know what to do with them. I remember working with one Scottish Premier League club some years ago, and the manager was quite a character; he was in the habit of weighing all the players to make sure they reached their target body weight. Unfortunately, he weighed them on a Friday afternoon, and fined them fifty quid if they were above their target weight. So the players would starve themselves to save fifty quid, and of course they couldn't play on Saturday."

Professor Maughan was refreshingly sceptical about the impact of a good diet on a footballer's performance. I quoted another passage of Wenger's biography to him, where Rivoire had written that "diet and food hygiene represent between 15 and 20 per cent of sporting performance at the highest levels". "No. No, no, no," said Maughan. "Talent is 80 per cent, and training's a substantial part, motivation's a big part, managing to stay free of injury's a big part, staying healthy is a big part; diet's a very small part."

"One of the things that's changed," he continued, "is that in recent years if you asked a player if he was fit, the player would just take that to mean, 'Are you injured or not injured?', i.e. are you available for selection. If you ask a track and field athlete, 'Are you fit?', the track and field athlete takes that to mean 'Are you at the peak of your physical performance, are you ready to perform the best that you can perform?'. That's not how the football player has traditionally looked at being fit."

Trevor Francis had known this all too well, as one of his former players at Sheffield Wednesday had told me. "What was good about Trevor Francis," he said, "was that he did bring a lot of the stuff that he'd got in Italy to Sheffield Wednesday: dieticians, things like that. I remember the first time a dietician came, the players didn't know what to do. They used to have egg and chips before a game, and they had this guy coming in telling them what they could and couldn't eat. They'd still go off after training and have a lasagne and chips."

Ignorance, though, was not confined to the footballers. Maughan dryly told me of a player at a leading Scottish club, of whom his manager had asked "'he's too fat, can you make him thinner?' Yes, I can make him thinner, but he won't be able to play football! What do you want? Do you want a guy that's carrying a few extra pounds, who's still perfectly able to run about the pitch for ninety minutes... Why do you want him to lose weight? Because he spoils the photoshoot? And the answer is, somebody's told him players should have no more than 12 per cent body fat; this guy had got 15 per cent. A little knowledge is a dangerous thing."

More vital than life or death

Bill Shankly made the most famous, or perhaps infamous, statement about obsession with football. The Liverpool manager once commented that "some people believe football is a matter of life and death. I'm very disappointed with that attitude. I can assure you it is much, much more important than that." Several years after his death, Shankly would be taken to task by another Liverpool legend. In his autobiography, the England winger, John Barnes, found it absurd that anyone could think that football was more important than life itself. Referring to the events of Hillsborough, Barnes wrote that:

> After each funeral I attended, when another set of parents buried a beloved son or daughter, when another grieving family mourned a relative who died following Liverpool, I would come home and climb into bed with my eldest son, Jamie, just to hold him, just to hear him breathing... Football lost its obsessive significance; it was not the be all and end all. How could it be when ninety-six people died, when parents lost children and children lost parents?

Barnes commented that Shankly's statement seemed "even falser" than before. And yet painting Shankly as a man devoid of any idea of what truly mattered in life seems an inaccurate picture. Looking at the devotion that the Scotsman showed to Liverpool's followers, it looks more as though he saw football and life as one and the same. Ernie Ashley, a season-ticket holder during the Shankly reign, remembered as much in an interview in *The Real Bill Shankly*. "I have seen Bill Shankly looking for people who were out of work outside different grounds, to give them a match ticket, as long as they wore a Red scarf. He had an incredibly close relationship with Reds supporters... on many occasions we would meet and talk to him on the train."

Karen Gill knew all about this. She was Bill Shankly's granddaughter, and witnessed his fixation at close (and, on occasion, uncomfortable) quarters. She'd noted that:

> That kind of total unswerving devotion to one thing demands a lot of energy and an endless supply of enthusiasm… it sometimes made people uneasy. My granddad did actually make some people feel as if they'd like to be somewhere else! [My grandmother] always said that if you didn't know anything about football you couldn't sit on your own with him for long. She would often sit in the living room of Bellefield Avenue racking her brains to think of some conversation opener, only to spurt out some ill-informed comment about some player or other, whereupon my granddad would launch into a long diatribe in order to enlighten her.

Gill's nanny, Ness, fared little better:

> My nanny Ness was often made to feel jittery as well, especially on a match day… If [Liverpool] lost it would mean days of stony silence at the Bellefield home. On one particular day, it was a derby day in fact, Ness had been unable to concentrate on her game of Scrabble and had rushed home from her friend's in order to listen to the match results on the transistor radio. She heaved a sigh of relief. It was a draw. That wasn't too

bad. A draw could be lived with, a draw could be endured.

Shankly, though perhaps a little too large for domestic life, was a man of the people; and if he'd been alive at the time of Hillsborough he'd likely have used football, as did Dalglish, as a means of uniting the city. One thing that football men have in common is their unswerving faith in their sport's ability to cure many ills. When, speaking to the former Chelsea manager, Bobby Campbell, he leaned forward and whispered, "You see, football – football makes the world go round." He said this with such conviction that I almost believed him. Or possibly just wanted to. There was something comforting about everything that mattered taking place within the four walls of your stadium, your most beloved of buildings. Watching the euphoria of some fans when their teams scored, you wondered if the last time that they'd been this content was when they were snugly tucked up back in the womb.

In their drive to succeed, football obsessives generally fall into two camps. There's the Bill Shankly camp, to whom nothing concerns them other than the workings of their own club. Their approach has both an innocence and an arrogance about it; they know that, whatever surprises the other has in store, they'll be wholly insufficient against their force and finesse. As Shankly himself explained – somewhat chillingly – "Our attitude was that if the football machine was working, the opposition might get caught up in it and get crushed by it." His focus was only on his players, their needs and concerns. Then there's the other camp, represented by Leeds United's Don Revie, who's like the school student who, in studying for his exams, takes just as much comfort from the revision that his classmates have not done as from the revision that he has done.

Indeed, Revie's preparations for each game were about as feverish as those of a swot sitting his finals. In *Don Revie:*

Portrait of a Footballing Enigma, Andrew Mourant wrote that "Revie's waking hours were riddled with phobias and rituals; taking the same route to his dugout before a match, a fear of ornamental elephants, a readiness to believe that a gypsy curse on Elland Road was preventing his side winning, even a distaste for birds in pictures or as motifs." However, his neuroses had other, less comical implications. Mourant recounts the tale of the time that Revie allegedly offered Bob Stokoe, who was the Sunderland manager, a sum of money in order to "throw" a match in Leeds' favour. "[Revie] denied everything," wrote Mourant, "though, while he initiated proceedings for libel, never went to court to clear his name. But Stokoe had no doubts. 'I remember the situation very clearly,' he said. 'He offered me £500 to take it easy. There were no witnesses. And when I said no, he asked if he could approach my players."

Reading this, you might have felt like telling Revie that it was only a game. Yet cultural historian Johan Huizinga would disagree. He'd point out that just because there was something childlike about playing games, that didn't make it any less essential in the course of our lives: "The consciousness of play being 'only a pretend' does not by any means prevent it from proceeding with the utmost seriousness, with an absorption, a devotion that passes into rapture... Play may rise to heights of beauty and sublimity that leave seriousness far beneath."

Fair enough; but not quite satisfying. Where did that absorption come from, I wondered? The question persisted: was there an enduring reason why managers were obsessed with something so apparently trivial as football? As I thought more about it, I realised that there might in fact be two reasons. One was complexity, and the other one was fear.

Easier seen than done

There are some disciplines in the world that look difficult at first glance. Like calculus, for example. The first time I looked at a blackboard filled with the dense scientific scribblings of Colonel Green, my maths teacher at prep school, I knew that calculus and I weren't going to get on. Green, a kindly man of green tweed jacket and stately baritone, was as bemused by my failure to take to his subject as I was; but, looking back, I think that calculus did me a favour. It was obviously hard to do, and thus there was no chance of me falling in love with it.

Football, on the other hand, has a deceptive, and therefore seductive, simplicity. "Hey, what's the big deal?" you ask, the first time you see a game. "It's just putting a ball in a net. Anyone can do that. How hard can it be?" Yet the most addictive challenges are those that initially seem easy, but are all the more *tantalisingly* difficult, the more you explore them.

Yes; perhaps the greatest beauty of football is the sheer randomness that lies beneath its apparently sedate surface. Rinus Michels, the Dutch coach named by FIFA as the Coach of the (twentieth) Century, has written as well as anyone on this topic. In his work *Teambuilding: the Road to Success*, he's visibly exasperated by the difficulty of the game, peppering his prose with exclamation marks at various turns. He compares football almost longingly with other sports that he sees as far simpler to coach. "Most sports have the luxury of one or more timeouts," he wrote, citing hockey and basketball. "On the other hand, the game of football is based on continuous action!"

There's one particular passage where, after writing it, Michels probably sat down and lightly massaged his temples with a cold, wet towel. "In the game of American football," Michels went on, his sentences a rattling crescendo:

There is only one player, the quarterback, who must, just like a football player, decide which option is the most team efficient one… the actions of most other players on the field are orchestrated by set patterns. This can absolutely not be said about football!… An accomplished football player must, together with adequate technique and specific mental and physical qualities, possess football intelligence, insight in the game, and recognize the ever-changing situation. He must be able to choose very quickly the most team efficient solution out of the many possible solutions. Talk about complexity!… in football, the ball is played with the feet…in team handball, volleyball and basketball the degree of accuracy is much greater when playing the ball. These games are less unpredictable!

So complexity is one reason why managers are obsessed with football. Another, as I've said, is fear: fear of leaving a world where you never really made your mark, or where you'd been so revered that life as a regular Joe frightens the life out of you. Jorge Valdano, writing in *Marca*, thought he understood the ambition of José Mourinho and Rafa Benítez.

They have two things in common: a previously denied, hitherto unsatisfied hunger for glory, and a desire to have everything under control. Both of these things stem from one key factor: neither Mourinho nor Benítez made it as a player. That has made them channel all their vanity into coaching. Those who did not have the talent to make it as players do not believe in the talent of players, they do not believe in the ability to improvise in order to win football matches. In short, Benítez and Mourinho are exactly the kind of coaches that Benítez and Mourinho would have needed to make it as players.

Well, Benítez and Mourinho might reply that they'd been doing something right. Unlike Valdano, they'd both managed their teams to a UEFA Champions League title, indeed Monrinho did so twice. Their obsession, if it was indeed rooted in vanity, had been a productive one for their careers; a deep-seated desperation to prove oneself is as good, if not as healthy, a motivation as any. By contrast, the problem was when ex-players became managers because they couldn't imagine a career, or even a life, outside the game. They were hooked on the highs and the lows of football, and they'd take any job that came their way, even if it was the hardest one that the sport had to offer.

Vialli, addicted

"You said it was kind of an addiction – it is an addiction," said Gianluca Vialli, somewhat ruefully, as we spoke about his career in football management. Vialli had had a mixed time of it; five trophies in five years at Chelsea followed by a sacking, and then to Watford, where he'd spent an ineffectual season before being dismissed from a three-year contract. "You want to carry on," he said, "and when you stop you feel like you don't want to think about the game after twenty years or so. You want to go on holiday and spend time with your family, and then you start missing it. You start missing the feeling. And it's why many former players want to get back into management – unless you find something else as exciting to do, or almost as exciting to do.

"It's so intense, and I think you need to be extremely motivated to want to be in the job. And I think it's unfair on your family, because you can handle the criticism and the pressure but your family can't. And you come back home and it's a 24/7 job, and you can't switch off, and it's nice to listen to your daughters when they have a problem and actually to understand what they're talking about – you're not thinking about 3–4–3 or 4–4–whatever."

Vialli seemed pretty relaxed that morning; he genuinely looked like someone who'd got football out of his system, who merely loved it and was not overwhelmed by it. He was about to do much more listening to his daughters in a short while – he was due to pick them up from school in just over an hour – but for now he'd made time, so that we could talk about 3–4–3 or 4–4–whatever. As the conversation progressed, I was fairly sure that he wasn't concealing any feverish desires to get back into management. All the same, I thought it wise to double-check that his obsession had gone, for the moment at least; and so I gave him the ex-footballer's equivalent of the lie-detector test. "What's your golf handicap?" I asked him. "Nine," he replied.

This was revealing. Four years previously, in an interview with the *Independent*, Vialli's golf handicap had been as high as 14; he'd clearly been walking the links quite thoroughly since then. I'd often suspected that you could tell how far an ex-footballer was from returning to the game – that is to say, how happy he was in his TV or other career – by the level of his golf handicap. Golf, after all, is a pastime most becoming of the retired player. It's something that Roy Keane would probably find as contemptible as the consumption of a prawn sandwich, conjuring as it does all sorts of images of self-absorbed corporate smugness, but a healthy golf life serves as a good indicator of emotional and financial comfort: in other words, a level of personal satisfaction that is the sworn enemy of a career in management.

Golf, football, and letting go

Looking at a small sample of some of television's most prominent football pundits, they all had either very good or excellent handicaps, indicating that they'd regularly been practising and/or loafing about in clubhouses. The BBC Press Office revealed that Alan Hansen, who'd frequently stated that he was steering well clear of management, had a handicap of 4.

Another website, listing him as one of their motivational speakers, had him with a handicap of 3. Gary Lineker's handicap was variously reported by the *Telegraph*, BBC Northern Ireland and FIFA.com as 6, 4 and 5. In late 2007, the most up-to-date figures I could find, the former Arsenal right-back Lee Dixon had a handicap of 3, whilst Jamie Redknapp had one of 9. Then, as Vialli noted, there was a footballer who had actually become a professional golfer, albeit with limited success: "That guy who used to play for West Ham, who had the dodgy knee, very tough." It turned out he meant Julian Dicks.

The pattern seemed obvious enough: those with handicaps in single figures weren't going to get involved in coaching anytime soon. The only exception to this rule was Alan Shearer. In May 2006, following his testimonial match at St James' Park – a 3–2 victory against Celtic, in which he had scored a late, staged, match-winning penalty – he told a crowd of 52,000 fans: "I'll be on the golf course trying to get my 6 handicap down." However, in April 2009, Shearer would exchange the much-mocked sanctity of the *Match of the Day* sofa for the managerial seat at Newcastle United.

Vialli, on the other hand, was not only content living *la dolce vita* of football punditry and clubhouse banter; he was also recommending it to others. "I'm a very good friend of Roberto Mancini, obviously," he said, "because we played together for so many years, and he's now coming to London, he's started to learn English. And I said the same to Marcello Lippi: I said: 'Look. Just be careful. Don't spend too long out of management, because you're going to like it so much that you will not want to go back to management! Because it's a different life! Look, we've got the financial capability to live a very comfortable life without working, and you can find the balance between excitement and boredom – and I think Mancini is not very far away from finding that balance!'"

(In hindsight, given that Mancini had just won three consecutive Italian league championships, or Scudetti, with Internazionale between 2006 and 2008, I should have asked why he was learning English; all would be revealed soon enough, as he went on to succeed Mark Hughes at Manchester City in the 2009–10 season. It looked as if the quiet life as recommended by Vialli would have to wait.)

"One more thing I would say about being a manager," said Vialli, "is one piece of advice I got from Alex Ferguson, and I totally agree with it: because looking back at my career – my very short career as a manager when I was at Chelsea and then at Watford – I was managing, I was doing my best, but at night-time I was going out with my girlfriend, I was watching telly, and I was capable of switching off. If you switch off, you improve your ability to observe, and to actually step back and realise what is not going well and how to change it.

"When I went to Watford, I was so into my role as a player-manager managing the club, managing the players, I got so *intense*, and I was always thinking – my attitude was, if I'm not thinking about management 24/7, I'm neglecting my job. And that is a mistake. You need to think about that 12 hours, 14 hours a day, and then you need to" – he snapped his fingers – "find something else to do; play golf, learn how to play piano, which is what Alex Ferguson did, learn a new language, play with your kids, go out, switch off. Otherwise you will lose the ability to observe, to step back and analyse the situation, and find solutions. Certain managers are too *intense*, and that's why they can't see what's going on." Perhaps that was the secret of Ferguson's success, I suggested; the ability to step away from it all? "Yes. He does that so well," said Vialli. "And he said that throughout his career, he got to a point at some stage when it was very *intense*, and he wasn't listening to anybody. He couldn't hear them talking to him, it was too *intense*." (My italics.)

Each time that Vialli used the word "intense", I could have looked back to Arsène Wenger on that touchline against Aston Villa, sinking deeper and deeper into the sandpit of self-analysis. That's a perennial problem for managers; assailed on all sides by suggestions from colleagues, staunch supporters and other far less friendly sources, they retreat so far into their own logic that their choices make sense only to themselves. Part of that, of course, is their own fault; the autocracy preferred by the majority of "British-style" managers – something we'll look at more closely in the chapter on Diplomacy – means that they've denied themselves that crucial room for breath and calm reflection. The art of good management is delegation; which is, not coincidentally, as good for your sanity as it is for the health of your organisation. John Faulkner told me the following story about Ferguson, football's foremost overlord, handing over some of his much-treasured power:

"Archie Knox was his assistant when he first went there, and he said that Archie Knox came in one day and said: 'Can I sit down and talk to you?' 'Sure, of course,' said Ferguson. 'I do nothing here,' said Knox. 'What are you talking about?' 'I don't take the training, I don't select the team; it's a waste of time me being here,' said Knox. 'No it's not, you're really helpful,' Ferguson had said." But, said Faulkner, Knox wouldn't be reassured. " 'I don't do anything. You do it all. Don't sigh – if it doesn't change, I'm going to have to go. So you're going to have to think about what I'm saying, and do something about it.' "

Taken aback, said Faulkner, Ferguson had begun to contemplate the departure of someone he regarded as a very good friend; and then he thought: "Yeah. I *do* do all the training, I do pick the team, and don't ask for much help with that either… " So, as Ferguson told Faulkner, "I called him back. I said, 'I've thought about it really deeply, and I'm going to give it a try.' Knox said, 'Alex, no. Giving it a try is not what I'm saying. Things have got to change. You've got to let go of some of the training and let me do it.' " So Ferguson said: "I did. And it was the best thing that I ever did. It saved my life... I stepped back. The coaching and the training was what I loved about being in football, and I had to let the thing go that I loved best. And it was the best thing that ever happened to me."

Visiting Bill Shankly

Whilst Vialli and Ferguson were doing their best to help managers to switch off, I was more interested in someone who'd been eternally switched on: who would firmly, and probably fiercely, have rejected all attempts to divert him towards the piano or the golf course. I was keen to look more closely at the obsession of Bill Shankly, a man so unnervingly single-minded that, upon his premature retirement in 1974, he was entirely bereft. Unwelcome at Melwood, Liverpool's training ground, since it was felt that his domineering persona would undermine the incoming manager Bob Paisley, Shankly spent much of the seven years of his retirement as a somewhat forlorn figure, away from the game with which he'd shared so much. Wanting to understand more about what had driven Shankly, I decided one mid-May afternoon to go and see him at home.

Of course, he'd died many years before, but I thought it would make sense to visit the place where he had grown up: figuring that I might, I don't know, find some of his essence there. It was a well-noted and remarkable fact that three of the game's greatest managers had been born in mining communities within forty miles of each other; Celtic's Jock Stein had entered the world in Burnbank, Lanarkshire, and Sir Matt Busby less than five miles south of him, in Bellshill; and, some thirty miles further south, there was Shankly, born in the Ayrshire town of Glenbuck.

Whatever Burnbank and Bellshill might have been, they now resembled West Drayton, the Greater London commuter town in which I'd grown up; but then again, all suburbs look the same after a while: functional, narrow, car-clogged streets, with the occasional respite of green. Like West Drayton, the people were as friendly as the towns were grey, which made for plenty of kindness and plenty of concrete. In Bellshill, there was the Sir Matt Busby Sports Centre, whose large sign had lost the last two words, so that as you passed by in your car or bus you would see SIR MATT BUSBY in your left or right window as you sped on your way. In the sports centre, however, there was no literature about the man; the only obvious sign of his association being a picture above the reception desk.

If there was little of Busby to be found in Bellshill, and even less of Stein to be found in Burnbank; his high school, Greenfield, no longer stood, and there was no sports centre in his honour. But that was to be expected. Given that Glenbuck was the most rural of the three birthplaces, remaining relatively untouched by modern life, I was confident I'd find the most answers there. Glenbuck, after all, had also been the home of the Glenbuck Cherrypickers, the local team that had produced fifty or so professional footballers – including Bill Shankly and all four of his brothers – between the 1870s and 1931. Whilst the Liverpool legend might have taken the path into professional football with an almost unhealthy obsession, it definitely wasn't a road that he'd walked alone.

My search for Shankly didn't have the best of beginnings. Before I'd set off from London, Glenbuck had looked reasonably accessible on the map. However, when I arrived in Scotland, it was as if the village had learned that I was intending to delve into the past of one of its favourite sons, and had become suddenly protective, disappearing from view. The receptionist at my Glasgow hotel had never heard of Glenbuck; she thought that I meant Glenboig, and so sent me ten miles on a bus in the wrong direction.

I then caught a cab, whose driver – despite having lived in the area his entire life – confessed that he, too, had "never heard of the place". Worse still, neither had his GPS system; when we'd informed the satellite navigation of our destination, it had pointed us in the direction of the inner city. With his professional pride on the line, Denis, a lifelong Glasgow Celtic fan, ignored the electronic guidance that we'd been given and headed blindly for Ayrshire. A few minutes later the GPS system, as if stirred by his commitment to the cause, decided to right itself and give us the correct directions; and so we rode on towards Glenbuck without further incident.

It spoke volumes for our destination that, although only 25 miles from the borders of Glasgow, there were lifelong inhabitants of that city who'd no idea that Shankly's home existed. In truth, too, my initial research into Glenbuck and its surrounding area had left little to recommend it. Thomas Findlay, in *Garan 1631 to Muirkirk 1950*, had portrayed the regional countryside as an untamed realm, frequented by feral beasts. "A Charter of the Monks of Melrose in 1176," wrote Findlay, "gave information to the effect that at that time the area was a wild forest land with animals such as deer, boar and wolves roaming its desolate wastes."

What's more, the neighbouring town – Muirkirk, just three and a half miles down the road – had shown its climate to be capable of the greatest austerity. "In 1740," related Findlay,

> a terrible cold spell struck Northern Europe… Muirkirk's own list of fatalities accounted for almost one third of the entire population of six hundred. The badly constructed houses could not keep out the freezing cold and many died in bed. Others dropped in the street or collapsed at their work. Farmers lost

practically all of their stock, the ground was frozen to a depth of three feet and the crops were useless.

These weren't endorsements to bring a surge to the spirits; but nothing that we saw upon our approach made us feel that they'd been fairly given. As we drove away from Glasgow, through Galston and Moscow up through Sornhill, we came upon endless beauty; from either side of the road, trees reached over to meet each other, forming high archways of birch and oak; and after Sorn, the landscape fell open into many miles of fields, springs flowing lazily alongside, and in the distance a range of hills steadily rising.

Shankly's hometown wasn't far now. Muirkirk came into view, and on a sublime summer's day Findlay's words seemed as distant as ever. More accurate were the words of the *Royal Commission of Housing (Scotland) 1913*, which had declared that "the inhabitants are a markedly good type... On the whole this is a good type of village. Very little trouble and expense would make it a desirable place to live in." Much of which made an impression on Denis, but not as much as the fact that, as he remarked, "We really *are* in the middle of nowhere."

From Anfield with love

Here, finally, was Glenbuck; tucked up in that corner of the countryside like a sleeping baby in the crook of her mother's elbow. A short steep walk from Muirkirk, Glenbuck – once a thriving valley, with coal quarried endlessly along its length – was enjoying yet another silent day. An ashen cliff-face led down to a wide grassy field, whose shade alternated between deep green and rich maroon. As Denis made his way back to Glasgow, having to put his faith in his GPS in order to escape from this hinterland, I went to meet with one of only two remaining inhabitants of Glenbuck, neither of whom were originally from the village. Where there had once been, at Glenbuck's peak, about a thousand dwellers, there was now only a Scottish lady and Kirti Mandir, a sculptor who'd settled there from India via Dublin and London. I'd contacted Mandir in the hope that a local artist would have as good a sense as anyone of the place and its historical context; it was a bonus, then, to be met with great hospitality and a generous helping of paprika, potato, fried onion and flaked rice.

In Mandir's home were a series of busts and bronzes, but he was perhaps most enthused about one that was on display elsewhere; he'd been commissioned to make a likeness of Robert Burns, arguably Scotland's finest and most famous poet, which sat handsomely in the town's museum. Mandir lived only a few yards up the hill from Shankly's memorial, a broad black headstone by the road towards the Glenbuck mines, which bore in gold lettering the words "The Legend. The Genius. The Man… From Anfield with Love. Thanks Shanks."

Placed there in 1997, it had been damaged in an accident a few years subsequently by some joyriding local youths, but – thankfully restored to health – it had had several other more respectful visitors. A local man came by twice a week to clean and polish the memorial and place flowers at its feet; there were also those who travelled from further afield. "Liverpool Football Club supporters worship [Shankly] like a god," said Mandir. "They come here by coach – so many people come to pay homage to him." For those hardy souls, this was a seven-hour, 400-mile round trip; showing that whatever devotion Shankly had showed to his fans, they and their children were repaying it in spades.

We were joined by Stuart Burns, a good friend of Mandir's, who had grown up in Glenbuck and worked in the mines for fifteen years; but who, smiling, quietly confessed that he didn't actually like football. Burns was much keener, though, on the history of his homeland, and, as he talked, Shankly's obsession started to make sense. There was something about the nature of Muirkirk, Glenbuck and the surrounding area that produced great leaders and innovators; not only had these few miles bequeathed Shankly, but also three famous inventors; William Murdoch (coal-gas lighting), John Louden McAdam (tarmacadam), and John Logie Baird, who gave us the television.

Having given me the rundown on these local legends, Burns drove Mandir and me down to the mines where he'd worked; mines that had now been replaced by the much safer and more efficient open-source method that was preferred by Scottish Coal, and beside which was a broad expanse of grass where the Glenbuck Cherrypickers used to play. Shankly had never appeared for the Cherrypickers' first eleven, but he'd have watched them play there in each spare moment.

Looking at those fields side by side with the mines, it made sense to put two other things next to each other, the most pertinent pair of statistics that, to my mind, Glenbuck could offer. The village had produced almost fifty professional footballers in fifty years; it had also seen ninety miners die in accidents over broadly the same period. Few people can have spent their youths with their choices in life so firmly juxtaposed. David P. Worthington, in *Bill Shankly – The Glenbuck Years*, wrote that "in 1927 the young Bill Shankly left school and found work in the mines earning 2s 6d (12½p) per day. After six months of emptying coal trucks Shankly found himself at the pit bottom and was later described by many of his colleagues as having a fetish for fresh air." As Shankly himself would succinctly put it, "There were only two things in Scotland in those days: the pit and football. Football was better."

The pit and football. Mandir had done his small piece

to immortalise the former, making a seven-foot-sculpture in homage to the miners who'd perished there; his Miner's Memorial had been unveiled in 2004 by Scotland's First Minister, a belated tribute to men who'd died pursuing a dying way of life. Meanwhile, Shankly had set about immortalising not only himself, but also a certain concept of football; one that, if not more than life and death, was certainly more than the mere game itself. For him, and for the other great managers – Stein, Busby – born within that narrow miners' belt between Glasgow and Ayr, to create entertaining football was a civic duty, a way of bringing light relief to those who were working harsh and arduous weeks in the darkness. It's fitting, then, that these three people who'd been faced with a life in the earth's depths did so much to take football to its greatest heights.

VISION

Let's imagine that you're the new manager of a football club, and you're riding in for your first day at work; and, whether you're getting there in your sleek saloon or on London's Tube, the chances are that you'll see your players before you see them. That's right; on your way into the office at one of the world's richest clubs, possibly before most or all of your team have risen, you'll have caught sight of some of them at least once, and perhaps several times. Look, there's your right-winger, hanging above the sleepy traffic; but despite the bitter chill he's happy enough, wearing nothing but a giant grin and a pair of decidedly snug boxer shorts. No player is bigger than the club, so goes the old cliché; but, at the moment, this player's clearly bigger than you.

And what's this? Your number 10's trying to get you to save with this bank, and your number 7's trying to get you to shave with that blade; your number 8's telling you to buy a car he clearly doesn't drive himself and your number 9, well, he's telling you to play tennis here, get your hair cut there, eat that pizza, munch these crisps, chomp that cereal, don that watch and quaff that tooth-rotting soft drink. By the time you see them all together on a Nike billboard, you're probably just relieved to see that they're actually still involved in football. Sighing, you might wonder whether your job is man management, or brand management.

Or let's say that the football club you're managing is a little poorer than that. Let's say that you're travelling to a ground ten miles outside town, to manage a team playing in the lower leagues, a club sinking even more swiftly down the table than it's sinking into debt. As you approach, the wind rushes over the arthritic joints of the stadium's gates, which creak open in greeting; as for the deserted, decrepit stands, the cockroaches have been hanging out there so long that they've got squatters' rights.

Onward to work you go. And whether you're on a bike, in a bus or a Bentley, the one vehicle truly carrying you forward is your vision. Yes: to be a truly great manager, you must have a dream. The dream needn't be as grand as Martin Luther King's; instead of the desire to hear freedom ringing from the Rockies of California and the Lookout Mountain of Tennessee, you could instead fantasise that, yea, one day Luton Town would return to their rightful place amongst the teams of the Championship. The dream need not even be as eloquently expressed as it was by Dr King, with his lyrical wish to see all the Earth's rough places made plain and its crooked places made straight: it could even be something so gruffly uttered as Sir Alex Ferguson's desire to "knock Liverpool off their f**king perch". But, at the very least, there must be a vision.

What Zola Saw

Some call it a vision; if you were Gianfranco Zola, the former Italy forward who'd starred for Napoli, Parma, Chelsea and Cagliari, you called it a project. The diminutive Sardinian, having retired at the age of thirty-eight, had worked for his country's under-21 team as an assistant coach before taking over at West Ham United in September 2008. It was here, having succeeded Alan Curbishley, that Zola set out his plans for the Premier League club. "The project," he told the *Daily Mail* in January 2009, "is to make a team capable of a high level. We cannot compete by spending £200 million so we have to do it through getting young players... Not all the time we will be looking abroad. We have good young English players here like Freddie Sears and Mark Noble and we are trying to improve them."

Three months later, having signed a new four-year deal, Zola felt sufficiently emboldened to enlarge upon his goals: "We are starting a project now, and the ambitions are that in a few years' time we want to be competing with the top four. That is the project. It's just the beginning. But we've lots of enthusiasm and we trust what we are doing."

I went to see Zola at Upton Park in February 2010; in the meantime, he'd seen plenty that could have scrubbed the rose tints from his view of the game. West Ham United had been besieged by misfortune, which apparently reminded the media of the bad luck suffered by the Egyptians when they'd rubbed God up the wrong way in the Old Testament. In the first half of the Bible, the Pharaoh had persecuted the children of Israel, and thus brought upon him and his people ten plagues, including infestations of flies, lice and frogs, rivers of blood, festering boils, swarms of locusts, and the death of the firstborn. For West Ham's sins, their plague was injury.

In the *Daily Mirror* you could read of the "injury-plagued [Kieron] Dyer", the midfielder once imagined as a successor to Paul Scholes in the England midfield, but who attracted ailments and ill-timed challenges wherever he went. The *Daily Telegraph* wrote of the "injury-plagued striker Dean Ashton", who was forced to retire at the age of twenty-six. Other "injury-plagued" West Ham players included the midfielder Scott Parker (*Daily Mail*), and forward Carlton Cole (*Goal.com*). That made four England internationals, each of them unavailable to Zola for prolonged periods of his tenure. Despite this, he'd finished ninth in his first season; but then, hit by the recession and his club's exposure to a series of poorly-advised Icelandic investments, Zola had found his club out of cash and therefore out of transfer-market clout.

I'd managed to see him at a time when "the project" had been in particular danger. Two days previously, the former owners of Birmingham City, David Gold and David Sullivan, had bought the club – then with a debt of £110 million – with a commitment to keep Zola in his job. One day earlier, a forward whom Zola had been about to sign – the former Chelsea and Barcelona striker, Eidur Gudjohnsen – had signed at the last minute for Tottenham Hotspur, having undergone a medical at West Ham. Zola, who confessed in the press conference that he felt "twisted and bitter" by Gudjohnsen's sudden change of direction, could have been excused for a somewhat bleak view of managerial life: after all, his team was only a few points from the foot of the Premier League table. What was it, then, that was currently getting him out of bed in the morning?

"The thought of what I'm going to do each day to improve my players; that's what gets me going," he told me. "I love it. I think it's the most important part of my job... For example, I like to get an individual player every day and work with him on a few bits. I think that, at the end of the day, the fact that you're just spending time with them and sharing your views, they feel better about that."

How Zola made his players feel better is something we'll return to later; but I was more interested in what had most troubled him over his year and a half in charge. To my surprise, he didn't mention plagues of injury or the club's poor financial performance. "The hardest thing for me was leaving players out," he said, revealing a compassion that I didn't readily associate with people in his position. "It was very, very difficult for me. Because when you see a player who is training very hard, and doing very well, and you have to leave him out… I didn't like that, at the beginning. That was a difficult part to get accustomed to."

At that time, Zola's project was bearing more frustration than fruit on the pitch. His team had a goal difference of minus 9, which spoke to an elegant but ineffectual strike force; had they been able to call on the services of an experienced striker or two, their league position might have been significantly higher. Like Wenger, a manager of whom the Italian spoke admiringly, Zola's charges were two or three years away from being players of widespread renown – players like the nineteen-year old Frank Nouble, a French forward acquired from Chelsea, and Jack Collison. The question was whether Zola would get the time to see that evolution. "It's a difficult job, obviously," he admitted, "because what you're doing is dealing with problems every day. The main problem is sorting out problems, and you need to be prepared for that… and you have to be enthusiastic about that. You actually have to love doing that." In fact Zola was not given the time to complete his project: he was sacked in May 2010.

Manchester United, a social club

As a manager joining an ailing club, you must both see and believe a road to your club's rude health that few others do; a quality that makes you not so much a visionary as a doctor. Coming to a club, a manager must make a quick, frank and forensic diagnosis of its ills; sensing any tensions, spotting any signs of decline, be they in the finances or the first-team squad.

Donald Rumsfeld, the former US Secretary of Defence, might have sympathised with the modern football manager. Commenting in an altogether different context, he showed a unique understanding of the difficulties of diagnosis. "As we know," he said in 2002, speaking about the military operation in Afghanistan, "there are known knowns; there are things we know we know. We also know there are known unknowns; that is to say, we know there are some things we do not know. But there are also unknown unknowns – the ones we don't know we don't know."

Rumsfeld, who went unloved by most of the world's liberals and indeed many of its conservatives, didn't receive much adulation for his remark; his critics saw it as a typically meaningless piece of analysis, as empty of content as the phrase "war on terror". But, looking past his ability to massage large quantities of salt into the wounds of friend and foe alike, Rumsfeld had a point (and, perhaps, a fleeting moment of humility). It's one thing to assess a problem before you; it's quite another when you don't realise that you're incapable of seeing the whole picture. There are occasions in football – the unknown unknowns – when a manager doesn't know where he should be looking for hope, or for trouble.

Sir Alex Ferguson, when he arrived at Manchester United from Aberdeen in 1986, had a great deal to take in at once. He'd been briefed in advance that several of the first-team players were extremely heavy drinkers, if not alcoholics; it might not, therefore, have been news to him that several of the players were unfit, ageing, and insufficiently robust for the demands of top-level football. However, he wasn't immediately aware that the club's problems ran deeper than this, noting only in his autobiography, *Managing My Life*, "the glaring inadequacies of the scouting system and the absence of a comprehensive and carefully structured youth policy". Ferguson's response, in the very next sentence, was to plant the seeds of empire. "My aim in management," he wrote, "has always been to lay foundations that will make a club successful for years, or even decades."

Having diagnosed the club, Ferguson then set about

imposing his vision. Another guru of management, the business writer and consultant Peter F. Drucker, once identified "the five most important questions that you will ever ask about your organization", and it's clear that Ferguson's intentions at Old Trafford were traced on a similarly thorough template. Drucker thought that each organisation (or, in this case, each football club) should ask itself the same questions: what its mission was; who its customer was; what the customer valued; what its results were; and finally, what its plan was.

The main issue was that, at Old Trafford in the mid-eighties, there was no plan. Manchester United, as Ferguson commented contemptuously, was "almost as much of a social club as a football club". This was shown no more clearly than by the training methods of the regime – if, given its laxness, it can indeed be called that – overseen by Ferguson's predecessor, Ron Atkinson. Ferguson received regular briefings from a former player of his at Aberdeen, Gordon Strachan, who was now at Manchester United. What he heard left him unamused: "The training, Gordon suggested, was a shambles with nothing done until Ron had a session on his sunbed as a preliminary to joining in a small-sided practice game."

It's unthinkable to imagine, for those born post-1985, that Manchester United could ever have been anything other than a dominant force in English football. In the next twenty-two years, under Ferguson's rule, they would accumulate over thirty trophies; including ten league championships, five FA Cups, a UEFA Cup-Winners Cup, and two UEFA Champions League titles. Yet in the period between the departure of the club's first great manager, Sir Matt Busby in 1971, and the arrival of Ferguson, United languished. At one point, they were even relegated to the Second Division in 1974, the goal that consigned them to this fate being scored by one of their greatest former players, Denis Law, who was now playing for perhaps their bitterest rivals, Manchester City. Their descent was as dramatic as that of Wolves, but it had been no less symbolic; it showed the lack of quality and continuity that leads to the fall of all empires, and which we'll look at more fully in the chapter on Diplomacy. For the time being, though, we'll get back to vision.

Knowing and selling your brand

Corporate-speak is something that doesn't rest too well on the tongue of the traditional football fan, and is generally spat as far away as possible. Roy Keane, the Irish midfielder who between 1993 and 2005 at Old Trafford established himself as one of the game's most influential players, showed his seething contempt for the business world and its creeping middle-class influence when he dismissed an unusually passive Manchester United crowd with a memorable rant: "Some people come to Old Trafford and I don't think they can spell football let alone understand it. They have a few drinks and probably the prawn sandwiches, and they don't realise what's going on out on the pitch." It probably wasn't fair of Keane to use the prawn – a tasty and inoffensive soul, though in need of a little garlic seasoning – as a vehicle for his disgust, but his view was clearly made. Yet, though he'd berated his fans for not showing the same unfettered intensity that he unleashed on the pitch, there are certainly times when football needs to be viewed through a dispassionate – and, yes, corporate – pair of eyes.

Football, at one level, is all about branding. After all, the key to establishing a successful product is working out its unique selling point. In other words: the best managers make the thought of playing for their club a prospect like no other, and they do so by putting their footballers in awe of the values and the history of the club. I saw this in an excellent documentary, presented by the former Liverpool player and Spanish television broadcaster Michael Robinson, who's returned to Anfield to feature the work of the brilliant forward Fernando Torres and the rest of the Spanish contingent at Liverpool. There's one scene of particular interest: Torres and two of his compatriots, the goalkeeper Pepe Reina and the left-back Alvaro Arbeloa, are invited to dinner with Sammy Lee, Kenny Dalglish and Graeme Souness, three players from Liverpool's Golden Age. (Liverpool claimed the European Cup, the most precious metal in club football, three times between 1977 and 1984, when Lee, Souness and Dalglish were at their peak.)

The conversation between the two groups takes place through an interpreter, which naturally leads Dalglish to follow the time-honoured tradition of all Brits who meet foreigners, which is to teach them the most vulgar expressions they know. Dalglish informs Torres, Reina and Arbeloa to their delight that he was known at Liverpool as the *cojones de perro*, which all reasonably laddish linguists will translate as "the dog's bollocks". The phrase has no literal translation in Spanish, and it's notable that the Spaniards burst out laughing before the translator hastily tells them that *cojones de perro* is a term of affection, and not an insult; but their initial reaction was fair enough, since it's a pretty strange language that, to convey affection, does so by comparing someone to a set of dangling genitals.

The meal's vital moment comes when Souness talks of the expectations placed upon a Liverpool player in the Platinum Age. "If we only won one trophy, it was regarded as a bad year," remembered Souness. "When we played, we were always made to feel as though we were never as good as the ones before," he said, as he gave Torres, Reina and Arbeloa a look that made them feel as if they were never as good as the ones before. The programme's subtitles describe the event as a "memorable dinner"; yet, although it was held for the Spaniards, it was they who were briefly on the receiving end of an inquisition.

To the credit of Fernando Torres, who was courteous throughout the footage and confirmed himself as one of the sport's gentlemen, he had a firm grasp of the Liverpool brand. "What I've learned since I arrived here," he told Robinson, "is that Liverpool is a people's club. The rest of us are just guests here." Torres, though a newcomer, had understood – perhaps some time before he had signed – that appearing for Liverpool had a rare significance; that the club's number 9 shirt wasn't just a length of polyester, but a mantle that you proudly assumed.

Huizinga, Wenger and the beautiful game

It's not for lofty academic reasons that a manager will encourage his players to look to the club's history. You can generally spot the difference between a footballer in mere pursuit of a pay cheque and one who's chasing a legacy; it's a good few more goals or clean sheets per season. As a manager, you're a salesman, and you're trading not in prawn sandwiches but dreams. You're continually selling your project, your vision, to your players and your supporters; and those who are best at doing so generally have a particular style in which they like to win, or a theory of play.

If you're still forming that theory, then the classic work on the art of play, written in 1938 by the Dutch thinker Johan Huizinga, has some good guidance on what it should involve. "Play," he wrote in *Homo ludens (Man at Play)*, "is free, is in fact freedom... Into an imperfect world and into the confusion of life it brings a temporary, a limited perfection... Play casts a spell over us; it is 'enchanting', 'captivating'. It is invested with the noblest qualities we are capable of perceiving in things: rhythm and harmony."

Huizinga's words suggest that there's a moral obligation to play games in a beautiful fashion, that there's more to any game than merely winning. Jorge Valdano, who won a World Cup with Argentina in 1986 and then went on to coach Real Madrid, has been more emphatic than most in this conviction. Writing in May 2007 in *Marca*, the Spanish daily, in the wake of the UEFA Champions League semi-final between Liverpool and Chelsea, he took Rafa Benítez and José Mourinho to task for the wholly defensive demeanour of their teams.

"Chelsea and Liverpool are the clearest, most exaggerated example of the way football is going; very intense, very collective, very tactical, very physical, and very direct." Valdano's words here were fairly temperate, but elsewhere in the article he reached for more vivid imagery. "Football is made up of subjective feeling, of suggestion – and, in that, Anfield is unbeatable. Put a shit hanging from a stick in the middle of this passionate, crazy stadium and there are people who will tell you it's a work of art. It's not: it's a shit hanging from a stick." Belatedly Valdano would be forced to eat his words; the 2008–2009 Champions League quarter-final between these two teams saw Chelsea prevail 7–5 on aggregate, a tie which saw goals that were far easier on the eye, or indeed the nose, than faeces suspended from wood. But his passionate belief – a widely-held one – was that football wasn't just about winning, it was about looking the part.

One of the keenest students of Huizinga's work was able to do both. Ernest Erbstein, of Jewish and Hungarian heritage, was one of the two men chiefly responsible for one of the most attractive and tragic teams that the game has known. With Leslie Lievesley he co-managed Torino to successive Italian league championships between 1946 and 1949. There was no team that could halt their supremacy; it was instead a cruel mechanical failure which would do that, as the plane carrying the entire first-team squad crashed near the town of Superga. Fortunately, visions of *Il Grande Torino*, as they became known, live far beyond their time. Immortality is the rarest thing that this sport grants you; it's hard enough to maintain your status from week to week, which José Mourinho ruefully acknowledged early in his career. "That's the way it is in football," he shrugged, during his time at the Portuguese first division side União de Leiria. "Today you're the best and tomorrow you're a jackass, and vice-versa."

It's easy to look like a jackass when you're grasping for feats that will see you remembered forever. Arsène Wenger has endured more criticism of his methods than most, but I always thought there was one particular image in his mind's eye that kept him going. His vision, I suspect, went something like this: a UEFA Champions League final in a balmy, distant, and wonderfully historic city, perhaps Athens; his Arsenal team 3–0 up by the seventy-fifth minute; 3–0, no more or less; 2–0 would imply that the game was not yet decided, 4–0 would suggest that the opposition was inadequate, and not really worthy of conquest.

And no: the team couldn't be a relative European also-ran like Bordeaux, it would have to be one with a fine tradition, like Juventus or Real Madrid. The goals would have arrived at regular intervals throughout the match: one from a carefully-studied set-piece, the second from a moment of individual artistry, and the final one from a bewildering sequence of passes, which would have drawn even the opposition's fans to rise in applause. And as his players celebrated this final strike, Wenger would look up at the stands, quietly yet excitedly watching the stadium clock as this night ticked down towards legend.

Wenger has apparently disputed such a view of his ambition, telling reporters on the eve of a European game against AC Milan in 2008 that "my objective is to achieve as much as I can for the club rather than becoming immortal. I know that no matter how immortal I become, I will die anyway. What advantage is it to you to be remembered after you're dead?" Wenger's dismissal of his own legacy seemed a contradiction when you saw his comments from May 2004 – with his team about to pass through an entire league campaign undefeated, winning twenty-six and drawing twelve of thirty-eight games – that they were on the brink of "real history", of "immortality". But, in reality, there was no difference between Wenger's desires and those of Arsenal. Managers like the Frenchman are at a club for so long that they become at one with it, indistinguishable from it; they don't seek glory for themselves as such, since they are as much part of the club as the cool white paint of the touchline or the paprika shakers in the Arsenal canteen.

Paisley the prophet

Men, or institutions, such as Wenger remain concerned for their club's welfare long after they have retired, and often have an unerring sense of how things will turn out in the long run. Bob Paisley was a prime example; he had been at Liverpool between 1939 and 1992, in that time playing for, managing and then acting as a director for the Anfield side. Returning to the medical analogy, Paisley had during those fifty-three years developed an acute awareness for any unpromising symptoms the club was beginning to display. In 1989, he became concerned that the then manager, Kenny Dalglish, was something of an inexperienced junior doctor, unable to see the subtle signs of wear and tear that were obvious to a physician of longer standing.

Paisley made his frustration clear in an interview he gave to the *Daily Mirror* in March that year, venting his spleen to millions of readers. "Liverpool are not the team they were," he warned. "They are not good enough just now and it's going to take a lot of money to put things right... [They] need more money to fund more top players coming in – but they're not going to get much for the lads who should be swept out. There are players who are holding up the progress of the youngsters, kids who should be coming through the reserves – but they're just not cottoning on."

Paisley would retire from Liverpool's board three years later, due to the debilitating effects of Alzheimer's Disease; his family considered that this uncharacteristic outburst to the *Mirror*'s readership marked the day that Paisley's condition began to worsen. Paisley's atypical lack of discretion may have sounded the alarm that all was not right; but the content of his words was nothing less than prophetic. Like so many terminal declines, that of Liverpool's reign was masked by a handful of dazzling, yet deceptive, dawns. Following Paisley's words, Kenny Dalglish's team would go on to win two of the next three league titles in 1988 and 1990, finishing second in 1989. However, for the next eighteen years they would go without a league title; worse still, they would finish second only twice, dropping as low as eighth in 1994.

A very Brazilian vision

Great managers very often see qualities in players that players don't see in themselves. Someone who knew that better than most was Raí, the legendary playmaker who captained Brazil in the early nineties and also starred alongside David Ginola and George Weah for Paris Saint-Germain. The younger brother of Socrates, an attacking midfielder of the rarest elegance for the national side, he'd had an equally prestigious career; and, as he was keen to relate, he owed most, if not all, to his coach at Sao Paulo, Tele Santana.

We met in West London just before his return to Brazil, where it transpired that he'd also followed in his brother's footsteps off the field, becoming a social activist. He was working there alongside Leonardo, his former international team-mate, for Athletes for Justice. He was also working in the corporate department at Sao Paulo, where he was revered as the finest player in their history. He didn't seem to have aged at all; though he was now well north of forty, he still had, somewhat disconcertingly, a full head of hair. Coming myself from a family whose male members experienced hairline recession from their late twenties onwards, I was a little bitter to see that his steepling black Afro had remained untouched by time.

Raí proudly recounted how he and Santana had won "everything" together, including the Copa Libertadores and the Intercontinental Club Cup twice each, in 1992 and 1994; yet he was honest enough to admit that their relationship hadn't started in harmonious fashion. Santana had come to town to find that his key player was ruling the dressing-room roost. "When he arrived in Sao Paulo," confessed Raí, "I was a little bit big-headed. I was the captain, I was the player of the match every match, and my head was like..." He motioned with his hands to try to show me the size of his ego at that time, forming a shape that was about the breadth of three or four pumpkins. "I was too, too comfortable."

Santana's challenge was to cut Raí down to size, and then build him up again; but having previously been Brazil's World Cup coach in their thrilling but ill-fated campaigns in 1982 and 1986, Raí was accustomed to a challenge of this type. "Sometimes he would drop me, just to give me a kick," remembered Raí. "He showed me that I could do more, much more." One of these related to his low number of headed goals; given that he was six-foot-three, he scored remarkably few. He drew a diagram of the long, late runs into the box that Santana urged him to make, which would be familiar to any regular viewers of Ruud Gullit in his prime; Raí did his homework, and the following season he was the top scorer in the Brazilian championship, with twenty-five goals.

Raí then outlined Santana's philosophy, which was based, it seemed, on the three Ps of passion, perfection and potential. "Firstly, he was passionate for football, which is the most important thing that you need. After that, he was someone that always went for perfection, with the group and with individuals. And he could see what [potential] every player had. Cafu is a very nice example of that. He was in midfield, but he didn't have great vision; but he had great potential [both] physically and technically. Santana could see that Cafu could use his potential much better at right-back; and it worked." It worked, indeed. Cafu would go on to become South American Footballer of the Year, a UEFA Champions League winner with AC Milan, and Brazil's right-back of choice for many, many years, appearing for them 142 times and in three World Cup finals – the only player to do so – whilst winning two of them.

Santana's vision seems to have been a joyfully blinkered one; in 1982 he must have thought that his attack was unassailable, and would carry his Brazil team to the World Cup. If he'd held such a belief, it would have been hard to blame him. His side scored thirteen goals in its first four matches of the tournament, at least three of which – 4–1 against Scotland, 4–0 over New Zealand, 3–1 versus Argentina – were 90-minute seminars in the footballing arts. Key to all this was Santana's assembly of a midfield whose names alone were hints as to the enduring beauty of their play: Toninho Cerezo, Zico, Socrates, Falcão, the last three in particular sounding like a list of long-dead and legendary poets.

But in the business of winning World Cups, poetry generally takes second place to guile. In the fifth match Brazil played in 1982, they were overcome by the pragmatism of Enzo Bearzot's Italy, for whom the Juventus striker Paolo Rossi would score a hat-trick in a 3–2 victory. Santana's team would be remembered as the romantic failures of the game, whilst Italy would go on to win the trophy, their first since Vittorio Pozzo's side had claimed it in 1938. Brazil, not for the last time at a major contest, had got their sums marginally wrong, figuring that South American style could outmatch European substance. They'd overdone it that time; but, as another long-dead poet, William Blake, once noted, "the road of excess leads to the palace of wisdom". Brazil would learn from their mistakes, and the next time they'd win the World Cup, their vision of football would be more measured, more deliberate; in other words, decidedly Italian.

Perhaps Santana saw the flaws in his team as the final proof of their enduring beauty; more possibly, he didn't see the flaws at all. Years later, he would remark that "All the best Brazilians were in Spain, I have a clear conscience on that. We just made the mistake of trying to mark Rossi man-to-man." At least, though, his team would be fondly viewed in years to come; fortunately for Santana, posterity smiles on beauty.

Rafa's eye for a player

It's sad to say, but sometimes you never quite realise the genius of a manager until you see how well his unheralded players are doing in your Fantasy Football League. Rafa Benítez has done exceptional things in his career; winning the UEFA Champions League with Liverpool in 2005, being runner-up in 2007. Immediately prior to his tenure at Anfield, which ended in 2010 with a move to Internazionale of Milan, he won two La Liga titles and a UEFA Cup with Valencia. Of course, I wasn't the first football-watcher to acknowledge his managerial gifts. But I never felt so humbled as a pundit as when I saw the player that Rafa Benítez had made out of Dirk Kuyt.

I never liked Dirk Kuyt. Actually, that's not true; I liked much about him, from his extraordinary work ethic to the clever lines that he ran down either flank, drawing defenders away from the centre of the field and giving his more creative team-mates vital room and moments in which to work. It's more that I feared for him. Benítez had signed Kuyt from Feyenoord for an undisclosed fee, believed to be in the region of £10 million; intrigued by his impressive goalscoring record, some seventy-one strikes in 101 games for the Dutch first division side, I watched him closely during Holland's World Cup 2006 campaign.

What I saw left me underwhelmed. Kuyt huffed and puffed about midfield, rugged and ungainly as a tractor. His team went out to Portugal in the quarter-finals, and he didn't score in the tournament; what's worse, he didn't really look like scoring. All I really remember was the sight of him charging towards the corner flag as if it were the Holy Grail. *Dirk*, you'd think, *the goal is that w– oh, never mind.*

Now, if you're going to pay anything around or upwards of £10 million for a forward, then he'd better be good at scoring goals – and not everything else except that. For a couple of years I'd lacked faith in the ability of Benítez to buy outstanding centre-forwards, which is why I'd been amazed at his purchase of Fernando Torres from Atlético Madrid. Before that, I'd seen him sign Peter Crouch, who'd never really convinced me – he didn't find the score sheet with sufficient regularity, netting forty times in 135 league appearances – and, at Valencia, the Norwegian John Carew, whose lack of touch hadn't really been offset by his strength and speed. Until Torres arrived for £20.2 million, Benítez seemed as if he was toying with the idea of buying pieces of the complete striker, instead of – in the forms of Crouch, Kuyt and Carew – frustrating portions of the genuine article.

But then I started looking at how Dirk Kuyt was doing in the Fantasy Football League tables; and noticing that he was consistently better value for money than one Steven Gerrard.

At mid-point of the 2007–08 season, with Liverpool at the top of the Premier League at the end of December, Kuyt had scored around ninety points, and cost less than £9 million; Gerrard's value was around £11 million, and had scored about 110 points. On a slightly more scientific analysis, there were the statistics that Opta provided in March 2009, shortly after Liverpool had defeated Aston Villa 5–0, with the aid of a hat-trick from Steven Gerrard.

Opta noted that, whilst Gerrard had taken most of the headlines in the Premier League that season, it was his colleague Dirk Kuyt who had created more chances per game from open play: fifty in thirty-one games, or 1.47 per game, as opposed to Gerrard's 1.41 chances created per game (thirty-eight in twenty-seven). Kuyt also led Gerrard in shots on target, excluding penalties and free-kicks, by 0.97 to 0.89. This wasn't to suggest that Kuyt is a better footballer than Gerrard, whose contribution to Liverpool's UEFA Champions League campaign that year moved Zinedine Zidane to comment that "he just might be" the best player in the world. But it made me realise that my vision of the game, as an armchair fan, was far more limited than I'd previously thought.

Malcolm Gladwell explains Peter Crouch

I think I was prejudiced against Peter Crouch because he didn't *look* like a footballer of the highest calibre. Players like, say, Barcelona's Samuel Eto'o were reassuringly aesthetic; the way they ran and carried themselves announced them as decisive footballers. Peter Crouch, meanwhile, seemed to stagger about like a newborn foal, but what did I know? He'd scored a perfect hat-trick – with left foot, right foot, and head – against Arsenal in the Premier League in March 2007, and numerous other goals on important occasions, not least a superb volley in England's 3–2 defeat to Croatia in a Euro 2008 qualifier at Wembley.

My poor judgement of Peter Crouch wasn't just down to the fact that I was a Manchester United fan; it was also down to what Malcolm Gladwell, in his book *Blink*, has called the "Warren Harding error". US President Warren Harding, argued Gladwell, was elected to the White House because he looked and sounded the part; quoting the journalist Mark Sullivan, who encountered Harding in 1899, Gladwell notes that Harding's "lightness on his feet, his erectness, his easy bearing, added to the impression of physical grace and virility… His voice was noticeably resonant, masculine, warm… His manner… suggested generous good nature, a wish to give pleasure, based on physical well-being and sincere kindness of heart." Harding would serve as President between 1921 and 1923, dying of a heart attack, but in that two-year period apparently did enough to go down as "one of the worst presidents in American history".

The Warren Harding error states that we look at people who are physically impressive and give them a free pass; we forgive them their faults, because they instinctively seem like the type of people who should be successful. It's the most common form of stereotyping, and Harding, if we're to believe Gladwell's analysis, was perhaps its greatest beneficiary. Though he may have exuded an air of integrity, it seems that Harding was something altogether different at heart. As Gladwell wrote, "Warren Harding was not a particularly intelligent man. He liked… to chase women; in fact, his sexual appetites were the stuff of legend. As he rose from one political office to another, he never once distinguished himself." Now, it's not clear whether Gladwell was pointing the subliminal finger at George W Bush as someone whose folksy and charming manner had everyone fooled. What is clear is that, at the end of the 2008–09 season, Sir Alex Ferguson accused the Old Trafford crowd of looking at Carlos Tevez and making the Warren Harding error.

One of the most drawn-out debates of that season was whether Manchester United would sign Carlos Tevez, the Argentine forward who had been on loan to them for two years. Were United to have signed him outright, he would have cost them an estimated £32 million, an amount that they had some reluctance in paying. Tevez was a footballer who attracted both frustration and fulsome praise; his play was punctuated with goals at crucial moments, but also with inexplicable misses. But he looked the part, almost excessively so; he flung himself over the turf towards every passing ball, vigorous as a man thrashing against quicksand. Such a footballer, a reassuring flurry of commitment, is the stuff that supporters' dreams are made of, and they were vibrantly vocal in their approval from the stands. However, after a 2–0 victory over Manchester City in May 2009 – in which Tevez had scored with a spectacular swerving drive – Ferguson remained largely unimpressed. Somewhat nastily, he commented, "The fans love a trier. That's the great thing about football. A lad who tries a lot can be forgiven for a lot of things."

Of course, Tevez would move the following year to Manchester City, something for which he would not be forgiven by several United fans. At the time, though, the Scotsman's observation had been dismissively made – that there were things, and more pointedly, faults, that managers notice that are beyond the ken of normal viewers. In that sense, it's fortunate that recent years have seen the rise of the statistician, to show regular football fans what they'd otherwise have failed to observe. Speaking with Duncan Alexander, the chief editor at Opta Sports, I saw clearly that the era of the unsung hero was no more. Opta provided statistics for Premier League and European club fixtures, and so they had a bird's-eye view of the players who were truly decisive; and they weren't necessarily those with the biggest reputations. As Alexander told me, "I remember – it was 03–04 – that the most creative player in the Premier League was Muzzy Izzet at Leicester. He had fourteen assists. And if you went through great names of creativity in the Premier League, you'd think of Beckham, Giggs and various others, but Muzzy Izzet probably wouldn't be one that sprang to mind."

Alexander also recalled that Jermaine Pennant, during Birmingham's relegation year of 2005–06, created more chances than any other player in the division that season; a sustained level of performance that was particularly impressive given the woes of the Midlands club, and which earned him a £6.7 million move to Liverpool. "You do get managers who in picking a player still rely on a hunch, [who say] 'ohh, he runs at fourteen the way that George Best did,' or something. But increasingly," continued Alexander, "I think managers are realising that to ignore the fact that this data exists, and that it can help, is foolish."

When to sell

Remaining on this tack, I spoke with Bill Gerrard, Professor of Football Finance at Leeds University, who was particularly well placed to talk about the increasing use of statistics in football. He'd been working closely with Billy Beane, who was the general manager of the Major League Baseball team, the Oakland Athletics (better known as the Oakland A's). Beane had been the subject of a bestselling book, Michael Lewis' *Moneyball: The Art of Winning an Unfair Game*: here, Lewis described how Beane – operating all the while within strict financial limits – relied on detailed analysis on data about players' performance to assemble one of the leading teams in the sport. For example, in 2001 and 2002, the Oakland A's had the second highest win-percentage of all thirty teams in the league during the regular season, despite having the second smallest and third smallest payrolls in those years.

It was easy to see why Gerrard and Beane were working together; like baseball, football was a national institution, and a sport that in many respects was stuck in its ways. Gerrard had spent a great deal of time working on the area of "managerial efficiency"; which, simply put, was the performance of the team as measured against the amount of money that had been invested in it.

Part of a manager's skill was knowing when to acquire players and when to release them once they were past their prime, so that they would represent little or no threat should they end up with a competitor. I asked Gerrard when the best ages would be to buy and sell players, but he pointed out that the issue wasn't that straightforward. "If you're trying to make capital gains on players, then you'll make your capital gains on players who you've acquired relatively young, and have sold by mid-career."

Gerrard continued: "The greatest gain in value for young players is those players between eighteen and twenty-five... that's where you're going to get the biggest appreciation, but like any asset you're going to get the biggest return where you've got the biggest risk. From the age of fifteen, sixteen, seventeen to twenty-five, that's where you get the biggest drop-out rate for players." He said that a significant number of players were culled out at the age of sixteen, as trainees, and by the age of twenty-one "around 85 per cent" of those trainees weren't to be found anywhere within professional football, in any of the four divisions. "Of even those players who get professional contracts at eighteen, nineteen," said Gerrard, "a third of them will drop out by the time they're twenty-one. So there's a huge attrition rate."

This element of risk – the knowledge that if you invested significant amounts in your youth system, very few would make it through in any event – explained why several clubs paid relatively little regard to their trainee programmes, preferring instead to buy the finished article from elsewhere. It was more expensive than bringing your own players through the ranks, but in a win-now culture it was overwhelmingly the safer choice.

Gerrard's analysis of player statistics was most helpful for smaller clubs who wanted to draw up what he called a "David strategy: where you accept that you've got limited resources, you can't compete with the Goliaths... so you try and do it differently. You try and get maximum efficiency out of your restricted budget."

A manager of particular efficiency – whose performance Gerrard described as "incredible" – sprang to mind; Everton's David Moyes, who that summer would go on to be voted by his peers from the Football League's four divisions as the League Managers Association's manager of the year. Moyes had won the award three times in all – his previous victories had come in 2003 and 2005 – and was the only man to have done so; in seven full seasons, his club had finished seventh, sixth, fifth (on two occasions) and fourth in the Premier League.

A look at Moyes' performance in the 2006–07 Premier League season showed just how effective his "David strategy" had been. In a league where, unsurprisingly, there was a strong correlation between a club's wage bill and its position in the final table, Everton had the ninth largest wage bill – at £38.4 million, some £10 million less than the league's average – and finished sixth. The only clubs whose returns were more impressive were Steve Coppell's Reading, who finished eighth despite the 17th largest wage bill (of £29.8 million), and Bolton, who under Sam Allardyce came seventh with the 16th largest wage bill (of £30.7 million). Reading would be relegated to the Championship the following year; what made Bolton's performance ultimately more impressive was that they'd managed to consolidate their place in the Premier League year after year.

Bolton had gone wholly unloved by the aesthetes of the game – as Gerrard noted, they had one of the lowest pass completion rates in the division – but that didn't unduly bother Allardyce. Whilst managers such as Wenger would publicly mutter about the negativity of Bolton's football, they might privately acknowledge that Allardyce was working as best he could with the meagre pieces of cloth that he'd been given.

ProZone

Bolton were a customer of ProZone, who analyse player performance for several of Europe's leading clubs; many of whom have, on average, three in-house analysts trained in accordance with ProZone's standards. Barry McNeill, their managing director, shed some light for me on the methods behind Allardyce's success at the Reebok Stadium. "When Sam Allardyce was there he was really the pioneer of a lot of sports science," said McNeill. Bolton, who were one of ProZone's first strategic partners, had requested a player rating system of significant complexity: this enabled them to deploy their players in unfamiliar positions to great effect. For example, there was the case of Henrik Pedersen, who was their centre-forward but who played at left-back for six games or so.

"[Pedersen] could only do that," said McNeill, "because Sam and the staff at Bolton had set his role up, and they knew that he could perform certain outputs based on his ProZone results. Sam played in such a structured manner that he knew that players in certain positions could perform at certain levels of ProZone data, be they physical or technical, to help them win. And that relationship has really now blossomed at a number of other clubs."

McNeill recalled a time, though, when clubs weren't so enlightened. "[ProZone] became the in-thing. Access became the competitive advantage, rather than effective usage. We had teams who would buy ProZone almost because it made them feel like a better coach." Perhaps, given that early experience, McNeill wasn't about to make triumphal claims about his product's role in the average manager's decision-making process. "Every team has its unsung heroes," he said. "I think, to be fair, a lot of managers intuitively know [who they are]; what they use ProZone for is to actually substantiate this to themselves, and then use it to communicate with the player."

ProZone's use, it seemed, was greatest when the manager needed to play salesman; either, in David Moyes' case, when he was convincing the board that a player was worth the money that he was asking, or, in Sam Allardyce's case, when he was suggesting Bolton as a possible destination to players whom he wished to acquire. His three finest signings – Real Madrid's Fernando Hierro and Ivan Campo, and Gary Speed, who was then at Newcastle United – all had distinguished pasts in the game, Hierro and Campo having won four UEFA Champions League titles between them, and so his pitch had to be an impressive one.

"One of the things Sam would do was show them ProZone and articulate the way Bolton played [and say] 'this is where I see you playing, this is what I see you doing'. And that in essence gave Hierro, or Campo, or Gary Speed the insight that Sam could use technology, he had a philosophy and could articulate it. As brand ambassadors, we were probably as good for [Bolton] as they were for us."

Campo was as good an ambassador for Allardyce's management as anyone. He would play for Bolton for six years as a defensive midfielder, having been signed as a centre-back, and he had been a revelation in that role. So grateful was Campo that, upon his departure, he wrote an emotional open letter to the club which the football journalist Guillem Balague posted on his website. Campo wrote:

> The time has come to say goodbye and I would like to bid farewell to every single one of you but, especially, I wish to convey my warmest and most affectionate wishes to Sam Allardyce. He came and found me in Madrid; he had faith in me and taught me how to be a better, more mature player. He played me in a position where I'd never played before in my life and that enabled me to see the game in a completely different light. I truly appreciate the faith he showed in me.

I found something uniquely affecting about Campo's words, which is why I'll end this chapter with them; because football management at all levels, beyond any considerations of titles, club crises and efficiency, is about seeing the best that players can be, in ways that might surprise even the players themselves. It's due to the wise eyes of managers that past legends of the game and those to come are put before us; and so it's to them, like Campo, we should give thanks.

CASE STUDY 1, VISION

TURNER'S TALE

The eye for a player

Some managers find themselves in positions where they have to bring once-great clubs back to health. Sir Alex Ferguson, at Manchester United, was one; Graham Turner, at Wolverhampton Wanderers, was another. In both cases, it was their eye for talent that pulled them from the mire; here is Turner's tale.

Graham Turner's itinerant career in management had taken him from Shrewsbury to Hereford, with a successful spell in the Black Country in between. Turner, looking back over his time as manager of Wolverhampton Wanderers in the late 1980s, described in a documentary the desolation that he'd found upon his arrival at Molineux. "They'd come down from the top flight to the bottom flight in consecutive seasons," Turner recalled. "If you can get defeatism into the fabric of a club, it was there. You could sense it… When I went to visit the ground, it was a real shock. Two sides of the ground were closed, [there were] buckets everywhere to catch the dripping water, rats everywhere; the place was a broken-down tip, apart from one magnificent stand on the one side. Gates were down to 2,000 or 3,000; basically, everybody had deserted the sinking ship."

Except Turner. There was something ghoulishly fascinating

about someone who was attracted to lost causes. Who were they, to think that they could resurrect legends? Wolves, as Turner had alluded in his interview, had once been England's greatest club; they wore gold shirts without irony, and proceeded to the top with ceremony. Between 1949 and 1960 their manager, Stan Cullis, led them to three league championships and two FA Cups, and once, in December 1954, even had the gall to declare them "the champions of the world". That month, his team had achieved a notable victory, albeit in a friendly match; they'd defeated Honved, the best side in Hungary, who in turn were regarded as the best footballing country of the age.

Cullis' claim therefore had a certain logic to it; what it didn't have was a sense of humility. The last time someone had got ideas above his station, the gods went and melted his wax wings; and so Wolves, having soared too close to the sun, duly fell faster than Icarus down the football league. Their name vanished from the high table of Leeds United, of Liverpool, of Manchester United; it was now to be found dwelling in more humble halls, with Gillingham, Hartlepool, Rotherham. And somehow, Wolves was even worse off than its new colleagues; whilst they'd long since accepted their proud places lower down the sport's order, Wolves had to cope with the greatest shame of all in football – faded glory.

I wanted to know why Turner had gone there, whether he'd walked in through those rust-mottled gates with a grand vision for the club. There was a compelling moment in his interview, when he'd spoken of the "one magnificent stand" at Wolves' ground, bracing itself in the face of the surrounding bleakness; that's where I thought I saw the romantic in him, as he smiled at this hint of what Wolves had been. Maybe, back then in 1986, he'd assumed this post with a vision of rekindling some of the joy of the Cullis years; perhaps, having been dismissed by Aston Villa, he simply needed a job. Either way, I thought that I'd go and ask him.

By the time I caught up with Turner, Wolves were a long way in the rear-view mirror of his career. That Friday, I'd caught four trains to see him, from Hackney into Wales and then out again, to an Army town on the English border; here, he was in charge of the League One side Hereford United, where he'd spent the last thirteen years. This meant he was sitting comfortably in second place among the Football League's longest-serving managers; between Sir Alex Ferguson (twenty-two years), and Arsène Wenger, who'd been at Arsenal a mere twelve years.

Or maybe he wasn't sitting quite so comfortably; within a few months of our conversation, he had resigned following Hereford's relegation. When I had visited him, the end was edging into sight; with about a dozen games to go of the season, Hereford were second-bottom of the third division, needing two victories to raise them into a position of safety. They were nicknamed the Bulls, and in Turner they had a manager appropriately headstrong. Having been relegated from the Football League in 1997, he'd brought them back up as a team of attacking aplomb, and then seen them promoted again, winning the award of League Two manager of the year in the process. Unusually, he was also the club's chairman, a role he'd taken in 1998 after Hereford United ran into significant financial difficulty.

By any definition, Hereford United were a humble club. This was shown no better than by my attempts to contact Turner, who due to his then dual roles was one of the busiest interviewees that I'd ever chased; when first calling Hereford, I'd asked if I could email Turner or his personal assistant, in order to request an interview. The operator kindly and promptly passed me his contact details, and I asked if I could also have the operator's email address, so that I could copy him into the correspondence. There was an embarrassed silence, and then the operator confessed: "Ah, er, the club only has one email address."

It looked like Turner had a taste for life at the sharp end of football. "It's not been by choice," he admitted. He had a particularly keen appreciation for the former greatness of his club; it turned out that Stan Cullis had lived in his road. His motivation for taking over at Wolves therefore came as no surprise. "The reason that I went in there was simply, as a boy, Wolves were my team," he said, although he'd not gone into the role with the fullest sense of the task ahead. "They were a broken-down club… it had become a joke. I went in '86, and it had been in receivership in '82 and '86. So the club was unrecognisable from one of the biggest in the world."

Nor had Turner's arrival been greeted with widespread rapture. Religion has generally treated its saviours with warm welcomes over the years, yet the world of football is a little different. With the exception of Newcastle United, whose supporters practically lined the streets with palm leaves when Kevin Keegan and then Alan Shearer ascended to the Tyneside throne, football fans are somewhat wary of new managers. Perhaps it's because, as disciples go, the football fan is the doubting Thomas of the pack. Try as he or she might, there's a lack of calmness or courage to believe in the leader's vision, especially when he doesn't quite look the part.

Lee Dixon, who played at Arsenal as a right-back between 1988 and 2002, told the BBC in a September 2006 interview that "Arsène Wenger reminded me of my school geography teacher when I first encountered him… I half expected him to have leather elbow patches on the elbows of his jacket." Dixon had tried to find out more about the Frenchman, but detail proved elusive. "I've got to admit that I hadn't even heard of Arsène when he was appointed to take over from Bruce Rioch… I'd tried to do a bit of research on him, but there wasn't much information available." Without any sign of the salvation that lay ahead, Dixon, like many a worshipper down the years, would just have to rely on faith.

For his part, Turner – who was then the fifth manager to be appointed at Wolves within two and a half years – recalls that "to be fair, I wasn't the universal choice for supporters; I wasn't the most popular person going in there." Discontent from the stands in a manager's early months can often prove fatal, and so Turner took swift steps to make peace with the Wolves' fans. "I think it was my first game [where], just to try to take the sting out of any unpopularity, I bought a big pair of gold earmuffs; so when the crowd started giving me a little bit of stick, I put this big pair of gold earmuffs on! I just thought it would lighten the mood."

The crowd's laughter, and the game's result – victory over Tranmere – kept Turner afloat; but what really allowed him to set glorious sail was his vision, which he was to demonstrate shortly afterwards. "It was hard work. We'd had a poor run of results; we'd got no money to spend until the chairman said that the owners were freeing up some money to buy a couple of players, or buy a player. So I went out and bought two kids: much to the dismay of the directors who'd invested £64,000 in two youngsters in West Brom reserves."

Supporters of West Bromwich Albion, Wolves' rivals in the Black Country, are probably recoiling with horror even today; indeed, it's almost cruel to remind them of this transaction. Turner had acquired Andy Thompson and Steve Bull; the former, a bustling and pugnacious full-back, would play for Wolves 431 times, whilst the latter would become one of the greatest goalscorers that the English game had seen.

Steve Bull would score 306 goals in 475 matches, his feats attracting such interest that he was called up to the England team for the 1990 World Cup in Italy, and scored four goals in thirteen games for the national side – a respectable record for any striker, made particularly impressive by the fact that he was playing in the Third Division at the time. Yet if he was so gifted, how had he managed to escape the eyes of the West Bromwich manager at the time, Ron Saunders? More importantly, what had Turner seen in him?

"With Steve Bull, you'd got just a raw ability there to get in goalscoring positions," said Turner. "Nothing would stand in his way, he'd trample over people to get into goalscoring positions. But he would need eight chances – seven of them would finish out of the ground, and he'd score on the eighth one. And when he came to us, gradually we worked on things, his percentages of scoring to the number of chances required got better; and he went on to be probably my best-ever signing."

There's no sign from YouTube that Steve Bull ever struggled to take his opportunities. Several fans have prepared online shrines to his genius, short films of highlights which show him nodding or thrashing the ball past countless hapless goalkeepers; he'd come a long way from when Turner had started working with him. "It was natural that he could get into goalscoring positions," said Turner, "but he wasn't a natural finisher as such. And then the quote came out from the top level that 'we don't think his first touch is quite good enough', and my reply was that 'yes, but his second touch finishes in the back of the net'." The team that Turner assembled, with Bull accompanied up front by Andy Mutch, an excellent attacking foil, took Wolves to promotion, and divisional titles, in successive seasons. Eventually, a few years after Turner's departure in 1994, they would return to the top division, now known as the Premier League.

This wasn't a return to the footballing heights of the Stan Cullis era, but perhaps it was just as important; it was a return to stability. Success attracts money in football, and vice-versa; fresh and extensive investment came from Sir Jack Hayward, who between 1990 and 2007 put £78 million of his own money into the club, and attendances increased almost ten-fold, the stadium regularly filling its current capacity of almost 29,000 seats. Sir Jack Hayward's vision was an invigorating one; but it owed everything to that of Graham Turner, one evening many years before, as he cast his eye over those West Bromwich Albion reserves.

PRESENCE

Five suited figures from some of Liverpool FC's most glorious years saunter towards the camera; and, appropriately, they're walking on water. It's a wintry day in 1969, and the Scousers are away from home. They're due to play Nottingham Forest at the City Ground, and they're making a pitch inspection before the match, traipsing over that crisp surface, with the gravel-crunch of frost underfoot.

One of them, arguably the hardest player the sixties has seen, is blowing hard with disbelief at the cold, his cheeks like bellows, puffed pregnant with hot air. Two others, oblivious to the chill, are strolling smartly forward; but it's the other two, central in this black-and-white shot, who truly catch the eye. One of them is leaning forward, the attentive pupil, as he listens to the master, the only man of the five who's wearing brogues and not boots on this icy turf.

Bill Shankly, stern and sharp as Frank Sinatra, is literally holding forth; his right hand's outstretched as he explains some thought or theory to Ian St John. It's clear from this photo who's running things, and it's as if he's surrounded by bodyguards: Shankly is flanked on his right by St John and Tommy Smith, on his left by Emlyn Hughes and Peter Thompson.

Judging from that picture, the one thing that Bill Shankly was lacking – relative to his players, at least – was height. The team over which he presided was as physically imposing as any that the game has witnessed. Not only did it contain Tommy Smith – half-man, half-granite – of whom Shankly once said that he "wasn't born, he was quarried", it also boasted Ron Yeats, who stood at 6ft 5in with the build of a blacksmith. Looking at Shankly in that photo, though, it was pretty clear from his body language that he didn't rule the Liverpool team through physical force. It's not that he wasn't tough – since he was raised as one of five brothers in a Scottish mining village, we can assume that he could handle himself – it's just that he had a way about him, evident from that photo, which commanded an instant following.

Charisma

There are many leaders, some more loved by the public than most, who've inspired this devotion in their disciples. Most obviously, there's the story in the King James Bible, in the second book of Mark at verse 14, when Jesus walks up to a tax collector and gives him a simple instruction: "And as he passed by," so the passage goes, "he saw Levi the son of Alphaeus sitting at the receipt of custom, and said unto him, Follow me. And he arose and followed him." When I'd either read or heard this in Sunday school, I'd been struck by it. People didn't get up and change the entire course of their lives just because someone told them to; then again, never having met Jesus, I hadn't had the chance to be overwhelmed by his charisma.

Football, on the other hand, would soon present me with such a figure, in the form of a brilliant young manager who'd worked in the Premier League; and it would be at a crucial point in my team's history. My team was the England Writers Football Team, and we'd just done something culturally unacceptable, which was to lose 6–1 to the Germans. A fair few people know of the existence of the England Writers Team, but far fewer know of this humiliation at the hands of our fiercest footballing rivals, and so a few paragraphs of digression by way of background are needed.

The team was one of writers who'd had a piece of work published, be it poetry, prose, fiction or non-fiction; it competed against teams of writers from other countries, and had travelled to places such as Norway, Spain, Sweden and Israel to take on its adversaries. The annihilation in question came when we were invited to a three-team tournament in Israel, which would be contested by ourselves, the host nation and Germany. As it was, the timing of our visit had a particular significance, coming as it did a week before the end of the Israeli government's ceasefire with Hamas.

Yet Middle Eastern politics has attracted dissertations from people infinitely wiser than me, and so I'll stick to football. We finished bottom of the tournament, losing 3–2 to Israel – having held a 2–1 lead at half-time – and then, on the following day, succumbing to fatigue against Germany, the score having been 2–1 until the last twenty-five minutes. Israel would run out eventual winners, defeating Germany 4–2 in the deciding fixture, while we were left to contemplate life at the bottom of the Western literary football world. (Admittedly a small world.)

Our situation called for some serious thinking, and so one of our players wrote an email to the League Managers Association, asking if a former Premier League manager could take us for a training session or two. The man whose help he'd requested was Aidy Boothroyd, who'd taken charge of Watford at the age of just thirty-four, and who'd taken them into the Premier League only a season after saving them from relegation to League One. Watford had lasted only a year in the top flight, returning immediately to the Championship, where their failure to secure promotion, along with growing disaffection over Boothroyd's long-ball tactics, saw him leave the Hertfordshire club after three-and-a-half years in charge.

I couldn't quite believe that he was coming in to speak with us. Maybe the novelty of the challenge appealed to him; perhaps he was looking for something different to do between jobs, since it was some months until he would be appointed as manager of Colchester United, a League One side. I didn't know for sure. What I did know was that, on the way to the ground, I felt a few moments of pathetic, playground anxiety. The media had painted a picture of him which, while not entirely unaffectionate, made him out to be something of an authoritarian. Most memorable was Ann Gripper's description of him in the *Independent* in November 2008: "A workaholic who has turned the mangling of aspirational management-speak into an artform, Aidy Boothroyd had long been the Championship's indefatigable answer to [*The Office*'s] David Brent."

I was therefore a little concerned. Boothroyd had watched the DVD of our defeat to Israel – mercifully, the Germany match hadn't been committed to video – and so he'd seen me wilt in the face of a highly-charged and compact midfield three. Of course, he'd seen ten thousand first touches better than mine, but I was worried that he might see flaws in my attitude. Less selfishly, I was worried that he'd be disappointed in us all, as we were far below the technical level that he was accustomed to working with. Though it went largely unspoken, I think most of our team felt the same. Writers are often criticised for being flakey types, with punctuality not being one of our core competencies, but we were all changed for training well before Boothroyd swept into the dressing room, armed with a whiteboard on which he'd scribbled a series of notes in firm and insistent capitals.

His performance – for there's no better word for it – was hypnotic. It wasn't his build that was remarkable: he wasn't particularly tall, or conspicuously broad of shoulder. Instead he was lean and compact, like an amateur boxer who'd never quite made the professional cut, but who remained widely respected; you couldn't see him starting a street scrap, but you could quite easily see him finishing one. His hair was short, but comfortably clear of military length; his lips were thin but not mean, his jaw steep rather than square, and if his brow had once been creased with concern over relegation, it now carried no such contours.

There was no one thing about Boothroyd that was remarkable; it was the cumulative effect of all he did that was compelling. He'd given a hint as to his methods in an interview with Brian Viner in the *Independent* in October 2006. There, he'd said that he was reading a book by Malcolm Gladwell, "called *The Tipping Point*, about the little things that together tip into a big thing, whether it be crime waves, flu epidemics, whatever. It's the same with a football team. You want the whole to be greater than the sum of its parts."

What, then, were the parts that left me feeling as mesmerised as Levi, the son of Alphaeus? What stood out before anything else was the respect that he had for us. First he learned our first names; he walked round the room, shaking us each firmly by the hand, looking us each in the eye as if he was raising a toast to our health. Then he showed us the first sheet of notes that he had written, and I felt a childish swell of pride as I saw the word "ENGLAND" at the top of the page; not "ENGLAND WRITERS", but "ENGLAND". Boothroyd had previously expressed a desire to coach the national side, but I was pretty sure he didn't think his big break would have arrived so early in his career.

What's more, his preparation was as meticulous as if he truly had been coaching Rooney, Gerrard and Lampard; having analysed our game against Israel in depth, he made minutely detailed recommendations for our attack, midfield and defence. There were diagrams and jokes, magnets and anecdotes. And all of this information was delivered in a tone that was measured, never hesitant, the sort that might stop a child crying or make a dog wonder if it really should be barking all that loud. He spoke for just under ten minutes, and by the end of it – well, it's embarrassing for a man in his thirties to say this, but he made me feel oddly safe: as if every football problem we'd had was going to be remedied, just you wait and see. "Any questions?" he asked, when he'd finished. There were none; he'd brought a room full of writers, England's most chattering of classes, to an awestruck silence. He turned and made his way out of the room towards the training ground; and, without a word, we rose up and followed him.

Football as religion, players as disciples

It made an odd kind of sense, if admittedly a blasphemous one, that a team of football players devoted to their manager might compare him with Jesus Christ. Most obviously, a football manager and Christ are followed by roughly the same number of disciples; and, like God, some managers insist upon omnipresence. In the Old Testament book of Jeremiah (chapter 23, verses 23–25), God – on typically ebullient Old Testament form – has the following words to say about the fact that He is everywhere at all times: "Am I a God at hand… and not a God afar off? Can any hide himself in secret places so that I shall not see him?… Don't I fill heaven and earth?"

Similarly, Auxerre's Guy Roux once commented that "I make sure a light stays on in my office all day and all night, like a candle in the church showing Christ is there". It might be that Roux was joking, but a closer look at the careful watch that he kept on his players left me not so sure. As Darren Tulett wrote in the *Observer* in 2005,

Roux is renowned for keeping a beady eye on what his players are up to off the field through a sophisticated network of informers. When word got back to the manager that the teenage [defender, Basile] Boli had a penchant for climbing over the academy walls at night, after lights-out, and whizzing around town on his moped, Roux took action. The next time Boli jumped the wall it was to find his moped chained to some railings. Monsieur Roux held the key.

Roux has been seen dragging players out of local night spots by their collars and been spotted at 7 a.m. with his hands on car bonnets outside players' homes to see if engines were still warm. With the bright lights of Paris just over an hour away by motorway, Roux recruited the toll-booth operators to his cause. Whenever one of his players had a night out in the capital, Roux knew about it. He even took to clocking the mileage on players' cars, just in case. A 400-kilometre addition one day to the next invariably meant the player had been to Paris and back.

Auxerre, where Roux managed for forty-four years until his retirement in 2005, is conveniently small for surveillance purposes, with a population of around 40,000. It proved the perfect place for a manager to remain abreast of his players' private affairs; it would have been interesting to see how Roux would have fared as the manager of, say, Paris Saint-Germain, where footballers could more easily disperse themselves among the capital's two million citizens. But, with his God-like omnipresence, I'm sure that he'd have found a way.

The swagger of Clough

We've established that for a manager to have presence, he doesn't need height; but he must have a way about him, be it serenity or swagger. The latter was best shown by Brian Clough in one famous, or infamous, incident. Immediately following his dismissal from Leeds United in 1974, after just forty-four days in charge, Clough was invited, or perhaps summoned, to appear on Yorkshire Television. There, he was asked to explain why things hadn't worked out for him at the Elland Road club. For the show – whose title *Goodbye Mr Clough*, pulled no punches – Clough was seated alongside none other than Don Revie, his predecessor, who had led Leeds to several years of success.

Predictably, it's electrifying viewing: in the footage Revie, who had gone on to become England manager, has apparently been brought in as the hatchet man, ready to call Clough to account for his spectacular failure. But Clough, the condemned man, sits there with the widest smile on his face, and answers each question with such joy that, at one point, I muted the footage and looked only at the body language of Clough and Revie; and, sure enough, it looks as if Revie's the one who's been sacked, Clough the one who's gloating over his corpse. Clough is infuriatingly gleeful, whilst Revie is ominously glum. It's as if they've just been visited by a soothsayer, who's told them both that Clough will go on to win not one, but two European Cups, as he would with Nottingham Forest in 1979 and 1980; and, in the same breath, told them that the best days of Don Revie's career are already behind him.

Even at Clough's lowest point in the interview – when asked by the forthright presenter, Austin Mitchell, how it felt to have had a vote of no-confidence against him by the Leeds players – he is strangely cheerful, almost euphoric. "Ohhh, I wanted to be sick; ohh, I wanted to be sick," grins Clough, as the camera turns to a visibly charmed Mitchell.

The early exchanges between Clough and Revie are almost friendly; Revie's facial expressions give no indication as to how unpleasant their acquaintance has been. This genteel piece of soft tennis isn't, of course, what the presenter wants to see, or is indeed being paid for, and so he politely invites the England manager to stick the knife in. "As an experienced manager, Don Revie," asks Mitchell, "what do you think was wrong with Brian's approach to Leeds as a manager?"

Revie replies: "Now, that's asking me to do something that I know nothing at all about. I've known Brian a long time" – his face giving no clue as to how pleasant or unpleasant their acquaintance has been – "what his approach is as a manager, I've never played under him, I've never worked under him; that is impossible for me to answer."

Further emboldened, if that were possible, Clough adds a healthy helping of smugness to the mix. "My style was exactly the same [as Don Revie's]," he says. "Management is 90 per cent [the same] right throughout the country, irrespective of who the manager is. It's the extra 10 per cent that's the special bit." The merest smirk that emerges when Clough finishes this sentence makes it very clear, if it wasn't already, that he thinks that he has the special bit.

Mitchell, the presenter, won't give up so easily though. He asks Revie why he and Clough don't get on; and, duly baited, Revie applies the scorpion sting. "I think Brian Clough is full of himself," he says, then going on to list an impressive roster of football legends – including himself, of course – whose egos he had bruised. Everyone's much more satisfied thereafter, Clough because he's drawn some bile from Revie, Revie because he's unleashed it, and Mitchell because he's provided one of the most compelling pieces of football-related television that we're likely to see.

Goodbye Mr Clough, on the face of it, was a programme about two competing egos. But, really, it was a programme about how difficult it is to inherit a legacy. There are many who consider that Clough, given the supreme achievements of Revie, was never likely to succeed at Leeds: managerial legends who leave clubs are only ever satisfactorily replaced by those from their own regime, as we'll see in subsequent chapters. Especially, that is, when their influence is as pervasive as Revie's. Of particular note in this context were the words of Billy Bremner, in a televised tribute to Clough's immediate predecessor. As Bremner explained, "[Revie] is Leeds United. When he was here, it doesn't matter if he was here, actually at the ground. He could [have been] in Scotland. But he was here; his presence was always here."

Dignity: Graham Taylor and King Kenny

What Revie also showed Clough was that a manager, if he wishes to be truly successful, must aim to embody his club, must have a sense of its soul. Guy Roux, in making his not-so-ironic comparisons between himself and the Almighty, had been on to something; he'd known that a manager isn't merely someone who runs a successful team, he is also its figurehead to the outside world. Getting a sense of this soul is no easy thing: you need to be alert and responsive to the desires of your fans, and the type of football that they want to see. The best example of a manager who really seemed to understand his club, to "get it", was given to me by Miles Jacobson, who told me a story about Graham Taylor, the former Watford and England manager.

Taylor was more famous for the embattled period he spent in charge of the national side between 1990 and 1993 than for his achievement in seeing Watford promoted four divisions in five years. This didn't affect his standing in the eyes of Jacobson, who swore by him as "the most amazing man I've ever had the honour to speak to". By way of illustration, he recalled a moment from his youth when "[Watford had] played against Crystal Palace. I'd saved up my pocket money to go to the game and we'd lost 4–1, we'd got absolutely hammered. And I was upset because I'd saved my pocket money to go to the game, and only one player on our team, in my opinion, had tried. So I sent a letter to the club, addressed to Mr Taylor, saying how disappointed I was... I had a phone call two days later from someone at the club, who certainly said they were Graham Taylor, and it sounded like his voice – I was quite young at the time, but I'm convinced to this day it was him – and he was asking if he could take the letter into the dressing room to show to the players. [I've got] no idea if he actually did it, but that's why I remained a Watford supporter."

Graham Taylor was clearly someone who, in Jacobson's view, had the best interests of the club at heart. But how do you know, as a manager, if you've made that transition from managerial new boy to trusted pair of hands? Perhaps you've truly achieved presence as a manager when your players, staff or the paying public give you a nickname that shows their respect for you. In his autobiography, Sir Bobby Charlton referred to Manchester United patriarch Sir Matt Busby as "the Old Man", whilst, in Sir Alex Ferguson's autobiography, he referred to Jock Stein as "the Big Man". Norman Hunter, many years after Don Revie's death, referred to him as "the Gaffer"; Rinus Michels was "the General"; and FIFA.com records that "the German footballing public knew Dettmar Cramer as 'Napoleon'. Franz Beckenbauer more reverently addressed him as the 'Professor', a mark of respect the Kaiser still uses today."

The pick of the bunch, though, is arguably that bestowed upon the Liverpool and Scotland forward, Kenny Dalglish. "King Kenny", as he became known, epitomised all that was best about the Anfield club; both on the pitch, where he won (among other trophies) six league championships and three European Cups, and off it, where he conducted himself with the rarest dignity. Though he had a public image as the most reticent of characters, he was brought forcibly from his shell by the events that took place at Hillsborough on 15 April 1989.

On that day, Liverpool were to go up against Nottingham Forest for a place in the FA Cup final; however, the occasion wouldn't be remembered for anything that happened on the field of play. Inadequate policing at the ground meant that thousands of Liverpool fans were shepherded through a set of narrow gates and turnstiles into a section of the stadium that was already full to bursting point; with waves of oblivious supporters moving in behind them, and with nowhere to go but up against the metal fences of the terraces or the chests of their fellow fans, ninety-six Liverpool followers were crushed to death.

Dalglish had witnessed such scenes not once, but twice before. In 1971, whilst at Celtic, he had been at Ibrox, Glasgow Rangers' ground, when a stairway collapsed, resulting in the death of sixty-six fans. In 1985, he would appear for Liverpool against Juventus in the European Cup final in the Heysel stadium, Belgium, on the same night that Liverpool fans would physically confront their Italian counterparts. In the ensuing fracas, one of Heysel's aging walls would disintegrate, falling upon and killing thirty-nine Juventus supporters. (Incidentally, at the time of the Hillsborough disaster, Liverpool were serving an indefinite ban from European competition, imposed due to the alleged culpability of their fans for the tragedy in Belgium.)

When he first heard, then, of what was happening at Hillsborough – he, with the other players, was in the dressing room when it all began – there might have been within him an appalling sense of *déjà vu*. Perhaps his experiences at Ibrox and Heysel had prepared him for the compassion that he would have to show at Hillsborough; or maybe nothing prepares you for what he would experience over the coming weeks, and to some extent still experiences today. As Dalglish wrote in his autobiography:

I don't know how many funerals I went to. Marina and I went to four in one day. We got a police escort between them. All the funerals were harrowing. All those families mourning the loss of their loved ones. Most of the church services finished with "You'll Never Walk Alone". I couldn't sing through any of the songs or hymns. I was too choked up. The words would never come out. I just stood there in a daze, still trying to come to terms with what had befallen the club and the people I so admired. The families were really appreciative that the players came along. If they had a favourite player, (then Liverpool director) Noel White would try to make sure that particular player was there. The last funeral I went to was as harrowing as the first. I didn't get used to the grieving. Every funeral devastated me, as another family bade farewell to somebody they loved and shared life with. As I sat at each one, all I could think of was how I would feel if it was my family. It was a feeling of "there, but for the grace of God, go I". I find it very difficult to talk about death. If the conversation turns that way, I immediately leave or try to change the subject.

Dalglish's daughter Kelly, in a March 2009 interview with the *Daily Mail*, revealed the extent to which he'd been affected by the burden of grief that he had borne. "As a teenager, all I remember is that he became snappy and awkward and different from the dad we'd known. One day he came back with two massive stacks of letters, many of them from the bereaved. One pile begged him to go ahead with the FA Cup semi-final replay and the other begged him not to. I remember him asking me in despair, 'What do I do?'"

His daughter continued: "My mum was brilliant and she made sure that life was happy and normal for us, but I know that she found my dad very difficult to live with during that time… A counsellor warned her to keep an eye on Dad and said it could be at least a year before he'd react to what happened but that he would react. The counsellor was right.

He developed a rash on his body, which lasted for months. He wasn't sleeping and kept getting headaches. It seemed to get worse at games, and he'd feel like his head was exploding to the point where he couldn't take it any more. It was like he had a nervous breakdown."

Of all the phrases in the paragraphs above, one stands out; that Dalglish and his wife attended four funerals in a single day. Four funerals, at each of which he would have to display a reserve and stoicism, conveying both a warmth but also a respectful distance towards people who days before could not have imagined being in his presence. He was there to inspire; but, at the same time, not to intrude on private grief. It was an impossible line to walk, and one that many might think was beyond the call of a manager's duty; but, in truth, it was entirely within Dalglish's job description. The contract that a manager has with his supporters is unwritten; there are all sorts of clauses that such a passionate relationship demands of him, and they're often only triggered at times of great pressure, when leadership – or more pertinently, presence – is called for. At Hillsborough, Dalglish did what no ordinary person – and, therefore, every manager – should rightly be expected to do. Because he saw that presence is simply about being there; no more, and no less.

STRATEGY

First of all, I should say that this chapter is written with begrudging thanks to Sun Tzu, the celebrated military strategist whose techniques dazzled the ancient world, and whose teachings survive to this day: his classic analysis of conflict, *The Art of War*, is still read worldwide, and with great admiration. I thank him begrudgingly because I don't think that Sun Tzu was a very nice man; but, at the same time, there's a persistent argument that the art of sport at the highest level isn't so different in tactical terms from the art of war. It's often suggested that the rigorous attention to detail, as displayed by the finest of generals, is something from which sports coaches can usefully learn.

Introducing Sun Tzu

On the face of it, there's not much that a football manager should learn from a professional warmonger: there aren't too many tasteful parallels between sport and slaughter. Wherever Bill Shankly is now – and his managerial record strongly suggests that, if there is indeed an afterlife, his soul ended up north rather than south – he will never hear the end of his statement that football was more important than life or death. Sun Tzu, on the other hand, had no illusions about the gravity of his work. Writing in around the 4th century BC, he lived in a period – the age of the Warring States – when a kingdom didn't last much longer than a snowflake settling in a muddy gutter. As noted by Samuel B. Griffith, the translator of Sun Tzu's work, this conflict "raged almost without ceasing for the next two and a quarter centuries… It is extremely unlikely that many generals died in bed during the hundred and fifty years between 450 and 300 BC."

In Sun Tzu's day, war and empire were big business, and, such is the nature of big business, that management consultants – for that's effectively what Sun Tzu was – were called in and paid large sums to advise the eager warriors on market share, best practice, and so on; how many more states they should conquer, that sort of thing.

During a discussion with Hö-lu, the King of Wu, on how the king might best expand his corporate interests, Sun Tzu was asked to carry out an exercise on the movement of troops, using the king's favourite concubines as commanders and a group of women as the troops. When the women, instead of moving as commanded by the concubines, burst out laughing, Sun Tzu had the concubines executed. He then appointed the next most senior concubines to lead the exercise. This time, "the women faced left, right, to the front, knelt and rose all in accordance with the prescribed drill. They did not dare to make the slightest noise."

In Sun Tzu's eyes, it was his neck or theirs. Griffith wrote that he belonged to a class of "professional talkers", whose counsel was widely sought, but who played with very high stakes for very high rewards. As Griffith remarks, men like Sun Tzu were "intellectual gamblers. When their advice turned out to be good they frequently attained high position; if poor, they were unceremoniously pickled, sawn in half, boiled, minced or torn apart by chariots." With pressure to perform such as that, it's unsurprising that Sun Tzu came up with the goods.

Winning at all costs

I've turned to the utterly ruthless Sun Tzu for help because there are those in football who find his teachings to be of great relevance. One of them is "Big Phil", known more formally as Luiz Felipe Scolari. Scolari, who managed Gremio to a Libertadores Cup triumph in 1995, and who managed Brazil to a World Cup victory in 2002, but who managed only seven months at Chelsea in 2008–09. During the Euro 2004 tournament, Scolari, as we're told by José Carlos Freitas in *Luiz Felipe Scolari – The Man, The Manager*, "returned to his favourite of many years, *The Art of War*... a text he used to support the players psychologically." Presumably, Sun Tzu's words carried some weight, as Portugal, the hosts, reached the final of that tournament where, alas, Scolari would find himself out-plotted by Otto Rehhagel, the manager of Greece, who led his team to victory by a single goal.

Retaining faith in Sun Tzu despite Greece's astonishing triumph, Scolari consulted him four years later. As Freitas writes, "For the opening game of the 2008 World Cup, [Scolari] again decided to use *The Art of War*, a justifiable choice given the fact that... it was a crucial match if Portuguese aspirations were to be met." Tzu's counsel again did the trick, Portugal winning 2–0, with goals from Pepe and Meireles.

Sun Tzu and Scolari were very much alike, in that they worked under great pressure to perform; the conservatism of their tactics reflected this. Their worldview was a far cry from that shared by football's founding figures. Although the sport's early years were frequented by men from Army backgrounds, from Major William Sudell at Preston North End in the 1880s to Major Frank Buckley at Wolverhampton Wanderers fifty years later, there was an unassailable amateur spirit that ultimately stopped its participants from taking themselves too seriously: this was reflected in the more carefree tactics that managers used at that time. However, the ready rush of cash into the sport soon changed all that, making the highest levels of the sport more and more insular and intense. A clear manifestation of this has been the growing austerity of the tactical landscape. When I spoke with the former Chelsea manager Bobby Campbell, the first thing he said, somewhat gruffly, was that they should "change the name of football to 'winning'".

In a game – sorry, business – where a manager's best players are being recklessly and incessantly headhunted, and where the senior administrators are doing everything to encourage the disloyalty of his employees, it's unsurprising that a manager should retreat into his tactical shell. After all, when winning is the only option for survival in such a volatile environment, then questions of the beautiful game often go out the window. This has led, in recent years, to cup finals being events of monumental boredom, the managers of both sides afraid to play flamboyant football in case they lose.

Take, for example, the 1994 World Cup Final. This game, in which Brazil defeated Italy 3–2 on penalties after extra-time following a goalless draw, was as low as I have seen football go. That's not because it was the worst game of football that I had seen – that would be the 0–0 draw I witnessed between Fulham and Derby County at Craven Cottage in the 2007–08 Premier League season, or England's 1–0 defeat of Ecuador on TV in the second round of World Cup 2006; on both occasions I fell asleep watching the match and woke up almost disappointed that it was still going on. No: it was the lowest point because it fell so far short of expectation.

We see these low points time and again within the later stages of the World Cup tournament: the quarter-finals, with one or two excellent exceptions (to wit, Italy's 2–0 defeat of Germany in the 2006 semi-final, or France's 2–1 elimination of Croatia at the same stage in 1998) are generally where we see the last of joyous football. Having qualified for the semi-finals, it's as if the players suddenly remember, "Ah, wait, we're at the premier international sporting event which occurs only once every four years and whose conquest we've been dreaming of since the playground."

In the 1994 World Cup Final some of the world's greatest attackers were on display, but they and their colleagues ended up shackled by either fantastic acts of defence, flagging fitness, or fear. Fear of failure was written all over that game, from the blank scoreline to the team-sheets. Baggio was plainly injured, but Arrigo Sacchi didn't dare to leave him out. Raí Oliveira was perhaps Brazil's form player going into the tournament, but he'd hit poor form early on, and so Carlos Alberto Parreira didn't dare to put him in.

However, when I spoke to Raí about his omission a few years later, there wasn't the merest hint of bitterness, but instead an empathy for Parreira's position. Responding to my suggestion that the Brazil manager had taken an overly defensive approach, he observed that "Parreira coached different teams in Brazil that had attacking styles. And if you look at the World Cup in 2006, Parreira's team wasn't exactly defensive: [he played] Ronaldo, Adriano, Ronaldinho, Kaká... But in the World Cup in 1994, when I played, Brazil hadn't won for twenty-four years, and it was big, big pressure. We had to win – twenty-four years in Brazil is a long, long, time. And I think this is the reason that he was obliged to be more defensive: we didn't have the right to lose."

That's perhaps the rule on which Sun Tzu and all professional managers can most heartily agree; that you don't have the right to lose. A march towards this conservatism was enabled by the creation of *catenaccio* (literally, chain) by Karl Rappan, who managed the Switzerland national team four times between 1937 and 1963. Rappan devised *catenaccio*, as

Jonathan Wilson notes in *Inverting the Pyramid: A History of Football Tactics*, upon accepting a simple but career-defining fact; that there are two types of manager, those who get to manage Brazil, and those who don't. As Rappan reasoned, "A team can be chosen according to two points of view. Either you have eleven individuals, who owing to sheer class and natural ability are entitled to beat their opponents – Brazil would be an example of that – or you have eleven average footballers, who have to be integrated into a particular conception, a plan."

With that in mind, he decided that his teams should play with three centre-backs, with a sweeper behind them, the thinking being that whenever a defender moved to confront an attacker, he would always have a spare man covering the space left by his advance. This system seems innocuous enough, but it led to football of exceptional caution. Rappan's teams, and others who adopted his methods, were in the habit of establishing early single-goal leads and then retreating behind their parapets for the rest of the match. It was a strategy whose effectiveness was matched only by the extent to which it was reviled for its negativity. The French-Argentine Helenio Herrera, for one, gave it a proud place at the centre of his coaching philosophy, and was rewarded with sixteen major titles in the course of his career. These trophies included, between 1950 and 1966, four *La Liga* championships and UEFA Cups (then known as the Inter City Fairs Cup) at Atlético Madrid and Barcelona, and three Serie A championships and two European Cups at Internazionale of Milan.

Presumably, Sun Tzu would have approved of this; for him, the tactical system was everything. Throughout his work, he never mentions a single soldier by name, not even to illustrate his arguments, or to describe the great triumphs that he's achieved. He's written a training manual for war, whose principles are timeless, and he'll be damned if any mere human is seen as pivotal to success.

In that sense, Sun Tzu and Rafa Benítez aren't so far apart; Benítez once commented that, whilst some players were admittedly more important than others, no player was indispensable. This has become an increasingly common view in football, but once it sat in a small minority; football, after all, is a sport which has survived for a long time on two obsessions, the cult of orthodoxy and the cult of the hero.

Sir Alf Ramsey: the system vs. the individual

The cult of orthodoxy is the oldest thing in the game, more ancient than the taking of half-time oranges or the ritual of the magic sponge being uselessly daubed over a player's broken leg. This cult insists that, even when you are using an unsuccessful system, you must persist with it at all costs. Familiarity doesn't breed contempt in football; it breeds contentment. This is a particularly English problem, which was encountered most forcefully by Sir Alf Ramsey in 1966.

That year Ramsey faced opposition, which now seems remarkable, to both his choice of formation and personnel; he'd decided to play 4–3–3, which over recent years has become the staple of many, if not most, of Europe's leading teams. For example, in each of three recent and consecutive semi-finals of the UEFA Champions League (2007, 2008 and 2009), we have seen each team use variations on the 4–3–3 format, a lone striker supported by two hard-working forwards breaking from midfield. Then, however, it was anathema; it was as if a renegade Christian had started trying to whip up support for the introduction of an Eleventh Commandment. Ramsey's creation was dubbed the "Wingless Wonders", and was looked upon with as much tenderness as the face of Frankenstein; victory, though, would vindicate him.

During the tournament, there was particular rancour over Ramsey's refusal to pick Jimmy Greaves, an illustrious but mercurial forward. It wasn't that Greaves had trouble finding the net; he would score forty-four goals in fifty-seven games for England, 266 goals in 379 games for Tottenham Hotspur, and nine goals in fourteen games for AC Milan, even though he failed to settle there. No; the concern with Greaves was that he didn't do enough defensive work, which left the team open to greater pressure than Ramsey would have liked. And so he selected Geoff Hurst in his place, who of course went in to score a hat-trick in England's 4-2 victory, picking up a knighthood into the bargain.

Meanwhile, the cult of the hero insists that whenever a team wins a great victory there must be a single identifiable talisman within the team: so, when Liverpool defeated AC Milan in the 2005 UEFA Champions League final, returning from a 0–3 deficit at half-time to win on penalties, Steven Gerrard won the majority of plaudits for his performance. Far fewer people were ready to recognise that the German defensive midfielder Dietmar Hamann, brought on at half-time to shackle Kaká, Milan's playmaker and chief author of chaos, was the quiet platform for Gerrard's effervescence.

Sun Tzu says: "Do your homework"

The study of tactics has often been a marginalised art form, traditionally something that many managers have indulged in after all other options have been exhausted. If a coaching session could be manifested as a meal, then tactics would be the Brussels sprouts. You only took them because you were told they were good for you.

Sun Tzu would have been horrified by such a view. "Determine the enemy's plans and you will know which strategy will be successful and which will not," he said, reasonably enough. However, those at the very forefront of the game would once have ignored him. Brian Clough himself admitted that "tactics played very little part in my method of management. I concentrated 90 per cent on how my team played, in preference to wondering about how the opposition would set out their stall. In other words, I worked, taught, coached, cajoled – call it what you want – all with the aim of getting the best out of my lot because, provided I achieved that, I knew that the opposition would have too much on their plate to surprise us. I didn't watch our opponents especially but I had *a rough knowledge* of them from seeing them on television… I didn't collect dossiers on opponents like Don Revie did at Leeds." (My italics.)

Clough's rough knowledge stood him in very good stead; after all, he won two league championships and two European Cups at Derby County and Nottingham Forest. With a record like that, it's possibly logical to argue that if it ain't broke, you shouldn't fix it. Bill Shankly might have subscribed to this view; his three league championships, two FA Cups and UEFA Cup with Liverpool were based upon player motivation rather than attention to minor details.

But there's another argument, which is that despite their monumental successes within the game, Clough and Shankly underachieved as managers, that their gloriously raw talent carried them through where men of lesser charisma would have floundered and fallen. That same argument states that Sir Alex Ferguson's record in European football with Manchester United, despite having won two UEFA Champions League titles in 1999 and 2008, was about two trophies below par.

It's true: winning the UEFA Champions League is nothing to be sniffed at, since it's a task that's been beyond many legends who've both played and coached the game. But Ferguson should have done it more often. Between 1992 and 2003, Manchester United were so crushingly dominant in their domestic league that they were the Rolls Royce of English football: they won the top division seven times in that period, their rivals probably wishing that they could have taken them to court for monopolising the trophy.

Yet, time and again, United's challenge fell away in Europe. The cult of orthodoxy covered up for them each time, masking the true reasons for their failure. The cult bleated that United should just keep playing their game, the 4–4–2 formation that had brought them so much joy in the Premiership, and success would come, year in, year out. Who in Europe could resist the four-fold midfield hurricane that was Ryan Giggs, David Beckham, Roy Keane and Paul Scholes? Who could repel the rampaging tandem of Dwight Yorke and Andy Cole up front?

Quite a few teams, actually. Of course, there was that uniquely thrilling 1998–99 season, when Manchester United won the treble of Premiership, FA Cup and UEFA Champions League; but, other than that, they wouldn't appear in the final until 2008. During that barren time – "barren" being a relative term, but only because United's enormous financial resources rightly create the highest expectations – the Old Trafford side were eliminated from the tournament on the away goals rule by unheralded teams such as Bayer Leverkusen (2002) and FC Porto (2004). Whilst these outfits were no slouches – they either went on to the final or, in Porto's case, won the trophy outright – the manner of the defeats, narrow, frustrating and marked by United's profligate finishing, gave a sense that Sir Alex Ferguson's team had ultimately beaten themselves.

Here, Sun Tzu knew something that Ferguson, belatedly and painfully, would come to accept; that, to win the closest contests, you can't go out there and impose your style on the opposition. You have to set traps for them. In what is probably the earliest endorsement of counter-attacking football on record, Sun Tzu wrote that "he who is prudent and lies in wait for an enemy who is not, will be victorious... Speed is the essence of war. Take advantage of the enemy's unpreparedness... strike him where he has taken no precautions." In this section, Tzu makes clear that, contrary to Clough's belief, you must do your homework.

Anti-football

Jonathan Wilson has also written that "the history of tactics, it seems, is the history of two interlinked tensions: aesthetics versus results on the one side and technique versus physique on the other." Thorough as Wilson is, we can see a third tension in the history of tactics: that of swagger versus sleight. In the early days of football, swagger was all the rage. You played for a team that had a certain style, and to hell with how the opposition wanted to play the game. It was all about you; it was all about dictating terms to the other side, overwhelming them with your brawn, your brilliance, or both. Real Madrid were some of the first and finest swaggerers of the modern era, who between 1956 and 1960 sauntered off with five consecutive European Cups. Before them, in the thirties, Herbert Chapman's Arsenal brazenly helped themselves to three league championships.

In more recent years, however, there's been a marked move towards sleight; defeating your opponent by stealth, through cuteness rather than brute force, confronting him only when he's exposed his hand. It's a new type of crime, and the tale of its emergence is partly told by the scoreline of arguably the greatest club performance of all time, given by that aforementioned Real Madrid team, who in 1960 defeated Eintracht Frankfurt 7–3 in the final of the European Cup.

This competition hadn't seen such a savaging before, and it hasn't seen one since. Madrid, led by the imperial Ferenc

Puskás and Alfredo di Stéfano – who, respectively, scored four and three times in the match – showed then and there that, if you wished to win major games, the emphasis was on attack, on outscoring your opposition. This isn't to say that defensive football didn't exist prior to 1960 – certainly, Vittorio Pozzo's World Cup-winning Italy sides of 1934 and 1938 knew how to keep things tight at the back. It's just that defenders were accorded a largely secondary role in football matters, their purpose being largely to feed the strikers with a healthy supply of ball; this is reflected in the fact that, until Herbert Chapman's intervention in the 1930s, many teams still played a 2–3–5 formation, with five forwards, three midfielders and just two defenders. Chapman's addition of an extra defender at the back, and the withdrawal of two attackers a little deeper into midfield, set the train of modern tactics in motion, so that, when we fast-forward sixty years, we find France winning the World Cup in 1998 with a triumph most notable for its defensive excellence.

During those sixty years, managers understood that, whilst their teams had mastered the art of scoring goals, they still had much to learn about preventing them. Even Rinus Michels, whose attacking brand of football still graces the daydreams of millions, grudgingly admitted that great teams must largely be built upon negative foundations. As he wrote in *Teambuilding*,

> Of the three functions within the team-building process – defending, building-up and attacking – the defensive team function has the highest priority when creating the correct balance in the team… *The anti-football process* must be taken care of. To not let the opponent get into their rhythm of play through being well-organized as a team is the basis for your own build-up and attack, and thus is a prerequisite to receiving the optimal result. To play efficiently and geared to the result takes precedent over playing beautiful football. (My italics.)

The anti-football process... Michels, perhaps all too aware of the heresy to which he is giving voice, ends the paragraph here, as if to take a deep and cleansing breath. Michels was, like Sun Tzu, the leading tactical thinker of his time; he was, to all intents and purposes, the architect of Total Football, the system that led Ajax to three consecutive European Cups between 1971 and 1973, and Holland to two consecutive World Cup finals in 1974 and 1978. "We have a hard time dealing with this in the Netherlands," he quickly continues, and shrugs, "however, this is the reality of football."

By the same token Brian Clough, for all his posture of being largely deaf to tactical chatter, had a keen appreciation of structure. He, as much as anyone, argued that every side should have a strong "spine"; his success rested on the simple formula, as he argued in his autobiography, of "centre-forwards, centre-halves, goalkeepers, in that order or in reverse order".

"Do as you are told"

Martin O'Neill, who played under Clough at Nottingham Forest, has taken this lesson to heart at each of the clubs where he has managed, be it Shepshed Dynamo or Celtic. George Borg, a successful non-league manager who made O'Neill's acquaintance at Leicester, recalls asking him why he was so successful. "Simple," said O'Neill, "I build a team." Borg then took out a biro and a sheet of paper, sketching out the skeleton of O'Neill's line-up. "He'll do his boxes," said Borg, drawing eleven blank rectangles on the page, two lines of four and then a lonely oblong at their rear. "He's going to play 4–4–2, he's not going to divert from 4–4–2," he said, jabbing briefly at the page for emphasis, "and then he will scour all the books [to see] who's available for the upcoming season, who's the best, who he can get on a long-term transfer.

And then he'll start filling in the boxes with his team."

Lurking beneath this dispassionate and straightforward format was O'Neill's scorn for the self-indulgent footballer, that free spirit who refuses to fit within or perform the role that he's been allocated. My enduring memory of the BBC's coverage of Euro 2000 was watching Martin O'Neill quietly fuming in the studio as his fellow analysts praised Francesco Totti. Italy's playmaker, felt O'Neill, wasn't being productive or decisive enough to justify the vast freedom that he'd been given by his manager Dino Zoff. When his turn to speak finally came, O'Neill's tone was calm enough, but behind his spectacles his eyes seethed with volcanic intent. "There's much improvement in him," came his terse voice. "There's much improvement in him."

Some managers will be especially punitive towards free-spirited members of their staff. Wu Ch'i, a loyal follower of Sun Tzu's ideas, had just about the nastiest way of dealing with those who disobeyed his tactical decrees. As Tu Mu observes in the footnotes of *The Art of War*, "When Wu Ch'i fought against Ch'in, there was an officer who before battle was joined, was unable to control his ardour. He advanced and took a pair of heads and returned. Wu Ch'i ordered him beheaded. The Army Commissioner admonished him, saying: 'This is a talented officer; you should not behead him.' Wu Ch'i replied: 'I am confident he is an officer of talent, but he is disobedient.' Thereupon he beheaded him."

Wu Ch'i did a lot of things like this. Most notoriously, he murdered his own wife to prove his loyalty to his clan; and so, when Scolari handed out *The Art of War* to his players, it wasn't this section that he had in mind. What Scolari might have done – and if he didn't, it would have been a nice touch – was to underline the best piece of poetry you'll find in any military handbook, since it gives players perfect tactical guidance on how to conduct themselves in a first-class football match.

As Sun Tzu encouraged his troops: "When campaigning, be swift as the wind; in leisurely pursuit, majestic as the forest; in raiding and plundering, like fire; in standing, firm as the mountains."

For a management consultant – which is effectively what Sun Tzu was – this is beautiful language; what's more, they're also words that José Mourinho seems to have taken to heart. Generally, his teams have been passionately immovable in defence, rapid in attack, accomplished at both containment and execution. Indeed, the Chelsea team with which Mourinho won his second successive Premier League title, in the 2005–06 season, was as close to complete as any that the English game has seen. Its individual members, though technically gifted, weren't quite as accomplished on the ball as the Arsenal side that had gone through an entire season unbeaten just two years before; but, as a collective force, they were an almost unmatched blend of force and, yes, flair.

The pendulums of José Mourinho

It's often said that Roman Abramovich dismissed Mourinho because he wasn't playing spectacular football, but there was much about Chelsea's play that year which was very easy on the eye. They won their first nine games, conceding only three goals, and scoring twenty-three. They also gathered some pretty significant scalps in the process, defeating Arsenal 1–0 and then, a few weeks later, decimating Liverpool 4–1 at Anfield. Chelsea's dominance at both ends of the field reminded me of two other teams: one from Italy, and one from the world of NBA basketball.

In 1995–96, Michael Jordan's Chicago Bulls – on their way to arguably the finest season of all time, winning seventy-two and losing just ten of eighty-two games – showed, like Chelsea, a total mastery of their field of play. Chicago had three of the game's greatest players: Dennis Rodman, Scottie Pippen, and the man who stood above them all, Michael Jordan. What was special about them wasn't only their live-wire athleticism, their lethal shooting accuracy from short or long range; it was the atmosphere that they created for their opponents. Being on court with the Bulls was as comfortable as shuffling barefoot over fibreglass. They never allowed the other team to settle; for them, the emphasis was always upon disruption, on buffeting opponents out of their rhythm. As soon as an attacker had evaded one obstacle, he was faced with another, and another; eventually succumbing to frustration, victim of a technique known as the "full-court press".

So it was with Mourinho's Chelsea. His team was arranged, at least on paper, in a fairly conventional formation; that of 4–3–3, with three lines between the opposition and Chelsea's goalkeeper. But, in reality, Mourinho managed to create a series of extra barriers between the opponent and the Chelsea goal by making each of his players occupy slightly staggered positions on the pitch. In attack, a snarling Didier Drogba would be the first to pound you back on your heels were you to move towards his goal, and if you made your way around him you'd run into two wingers, one of whom, Joe Cole, was small but could tackle with surprising spite.

Having advanced, you'd find more trouble. Instead of Mourinho's three central midfielders – Frank Lampard, Michael Essien and Claude Makélélé – standing shoulder-to-shoulder, each of them stood progressively deeper than the other, so that instead of facing one defensive screen, you were now facing three. The same applied to the centre-backs: John Terry and William Gallas stood a few steps off each other, one making the first challenge on you and the other sweeping up the stray ball that might bounce his way. Finally, you'd confront the goalkeeper Petr Cech, who was so colossal a presence that you could have sworn that he'd secretly swapped his full-size goal for a five-a-side net. In short, were you to run towards Chelsea's penalty area, your journey would feel less like a football match and more like a raid on a cave to make off with a furiously guarded ancient treasure.

Mourinho's all conquering Inter Milan team of 2009–10 showed the same defensive resilience combined with moments of counter-attacking brilliance. Mourinho's brand of defensive intensity, where a succession of players swung like a flurry of pendulums before you as you approached, was football's equivalent of the full-court press. He was one of the firmest advocates of this tactic which was so successfully pioneered by AC Milan's Arrigo Sacchi in the late 1980s. He also showed himself to be a great fan of the ultimate form of theft, of sneaking in behind the other team's defences, which is the counter-attack; or, to use the technical term, "transition". As Mourinho commented in UEFA's analysis of the 2007–08 UEFA Champions League season, "quick transition is the most important aspect in the UEFA Champions League – quickly restructuring to defend, or exploiting the opponent with speed when the ball is regained. Of course, set plays matter, but transition speed is vital."

Arsène Wenger, Mourinho's virulent rival on so many other occasions, agrees with him here, considering that "the two key elements in the UEFA Champions League are the transition speed, and from a coaching perspective, the last ten to fifteen minutes". Transition also provided the most eye-catching statistic in UEFA's Technical Report for the Euro 2008 tournament. "Approximately 46 per cent of the goals scored in open play stemmed from fast breaks or counter-attacks," revealed UEFA. "With some of the set-play goals also originating from counters, it means that around half of the goals were down to quick and effective use of the ball as soon as it was won. This represented a very high return."

Marcello Lippi's Juventus, who reached three successive

Champions League finals in the mid-to-late 1990s, winning one against Ajax in 1996, were masters of the art of transition: they had fast, sharp passing, and an attack that variously featured Alessandro Del Piero, Zinedine Zidane and Gianluca Vialli. The problem that the Turin side faced was that, confronted with a team-sheet as good as theirs, opposition teams would arrive at the Stadio delle Alpi and defend for ninety minutes; as Mourinho would phrase it, they would "park a bus" in front of their goal. Juventus therefore had to find a way to tempt their shy visitors out into the open where they could summarily overcome them. Luckily, they had the patience and the nous for such a task; in other words, they knew how to play "circulation football".

Football in your team's blood

In *Teambuilding*, Rinus Michels writes that "circulation football is the name for a specific build-up style… This strategy is distinguished by the ability to circulate the ball from player to player until the correct moment arises for the attacking phase and thus, the ball can be played deep." Michels also notes that "not many top teams master this well", naming France, Brazil, Barcelona and – to his own surprise – England as coached by Glenn Hoddle in World Cup 1998, as the sides that had exhibited rare mastery of this technique.

Michels' choice of metaphor is interesting here. He writes of circulation, which gives a sense of the ball coursing through the team's bloodstream, biding its time in cooler veins before darting through arteries towards its eventual target. But, with all respect, it doesn't quite capture the elegant deliberation of the football that Michels describes. When he discusses "circulation football" it instead conjures up an unfortunate image of a rush of blood, which is precisely the sort of frantic style that Michels expected, not without justification, from the English national team. No: watching perhaps the most mesmeric example of Michels' "circulation football" that I had ever seen, it reminded me more of mountain climbing than anything else.

The example – or, more accurately, the exhibition – was given by Barcelona, on their visit to Anfield for a UEFA Champions League group match in November 2001. Liverpool, then coached by Gérard Houllier, had taken the lead through Michael Owen. Barcelona, managed by their former player Carles Rexach, responded with goals from Patrick Kluivert and Fabio Rochemback, and for their third and final strike, they climbed a mountain.

With just under nine minutes of the match to go, Liverpool lose possession of the ball just into Barcelona's half. The home side will only touch the ball twice more in the next three minutes; the first time, to make a clearing tackle out on their frantic right flank, and the second time, inevitably, to retrieve it from their own net. When Barcelona take the ball, looking at how they can break down the Liverpool defence, it's as if they're caressing the contours of a sheer cliff-face, wondering where they should first place their footholds before they make that sudden and steep ascent.

Faced by a steady line of defence, Barcelona calmly pass their hands over the stubborn surface, working the ball with one, two, three touches at a time across the width and the depth of the pitch. The first time, after a sequence of thirty-one passes, they stumble back to earth: they try to scale the heights too soon, Kluivert attempting to roam where there's no room for him, and the ball's thrashed clear by Sami Hyppia, the trenchant Liverpool centre-back. But the second time, Barcelona are a little more patient, and this time they reach the summit.

From their throw-in, they first push the ball forward, then sweep it back, back, back into their own half: they've taken the ball to the mountain once, and failed, so now the mountain must come to them. They move the ball across the field, either chipped, clipped or prodded away from the toes of advancing Liverpool players, until very swiftly the path to goal becomes clear, and it's only then that the twenty-eighth and final pass is played, stroked by Xavi beyond the last defender to the Dutch winger Marc Overmars. Overmars, though in the last orders phase of his career, is still thoroughly uncatchable, and shimmies past the forlorn Jerzy Dudek in the Liverpool goal: 3–1. Michels, were he watching the game that night, must have nodded in approval.

Circulation football, as supremely demonstrated by the Catalans, is alive and well at the highest level of the game. This is shown by the prevalence of the sideways pass, or the "square ball", in the UEFA Champions League; a pass that's played to retain possession, when there's no direct attacking option available. According to ProZone, the UEFA Champions League has the highest proportion of square passes, at 37 per cent; that's comfortably ahead of the Premier League, for example, where that figure is 32 per cent.

Unsurprisingly, circulation football is also the stock in trade of Juventus. Yet a curiosity of their play was that they would routinely outclass teams, yet defeat them only 1–0. I never really understood this until I watched Pete Sampras, the American tennis legend, with some regularity, and saw that he'd taken a leaf from the same book as Lippi. Why waste energy in trying to thrash your opponent 6–0, 6–0, 6–0 when you could patiently rally with him, let him hold his serve for a few games, and then break him at the end of each set?

Momentum

Moreover, looking at modern football – and, specifically, at the 2006 World Cup – one break is generally all you'll need.

Three of the four teams in this tournament's semi-finals – France, Portugal and eventual winners Italy – played with a single forward who, as we've seen from the earlier example of Serie A, was liable to wander about up front as lonely as Wordsworth's cloud. In FIFA's technical report on this competition, they noted that

in forty-one of the sixty-four matches played… the team that scored the opening goal went on to win the game. As there were also seven goalless draws and eight games in which the team that went 1–0 down managed to level the scores, there were only eight matches in which a team came from behind to win. This psychological aspect of a lead was doubtless the principal reason why teams were anxious not to go behind and thus generally operated with a solid defence.

To know when to deal the killer-blow is a matter of immaculate timing, in football as in tennis. However, whilst tennis has a readily recognisable moment when you should attempt to strike – at four games all, say, or when you're five points apiece in a tie-break – football doesn't so easily signpost the turning points in each match. A manager must have a sense, whether innate or acquired, of when a game's at a crucial point; in other words, he must have an understanding of momentum, a topic to which the Football Association has devoted a manual, *Momentum in Soccer: Controlling the Game*, all of its own.

As the manual explained at its outset, straying vaguely into the territory of Eastern mysticism:

Momentum is the force that dictates the flow of a match: a hidden force because it is not always reflected in the score. It is invisible because it comes from the flow of energy between competitors that, in turn, affects their performance on the pitch. A player or spectator can *feel* things going for or against him or the team he is watching, *sensing* who holds the balance of power at key moments in the match. The flow of momentum

> creates the pattern of the match. It makes matches ebb and flow. (Their italics.)

Italian managers have traditionally understood this better than any of their counterparts. The Frenchman Marcel Desailly was well versed in tactical cuteness, having starred as both a centre-back and defensive midfielder for AC Milan; he once observed that in Serie A, teams were only expected to play for sixty of the ninety minutes, the rest of the while keeping their movement deliberately downbeat. In *Momentum in Soccer*, Gianluca Vialli, whose career in Serie A roughly overlapped with that of Desailly, noted the relative honesty – or naivety – of the English approach. Vialli observed that:

> In England the way you tackle is different, it is very honest, you go for the ball… If you win, you get it and if you don't, their team may get it. But in Italy the attitude is, "I could go for the ball and yes, I might get it, but if I miss it, well, they might get past me and hurt us," so the priority is first and foremost not to get hurt tactically. And often you see that if they go past them they foul the player and you will see that there are a lot more tactical fouls. Some managers have been known to say that, "in the statistics we only made fifty fouls; we need to make seventy-five fouls, in order to win the game; tactical fouls".

I'd always suspected that time-wasting of this nature was a general tactic, but was still surprised to see that it was planned with such precision; and, to be honest, a little annoyed, cheated perhaps. This didn't seem how football was meant to be played: football was meant to be a thrillingly continuous contest, not some sluggish stalemate whose midfield was policed by the sporting equivalent of traffic wardens.

I'd watched coverage of Serie A many times during the period in the 1990s when it was screened on Channel 4, and each game seemed to follow almost precisely the same pattern; if the home team didn't score within the first twenty minutes, then the game would very likely finish as a goalless draw. This was because the visiting team had generally come in search of a point, and made no bones about that fact; they would typically play with four defenders, five unadventurous midfielders, and a single forward, who looked so morose that you wondered if they'd simply stuck him there to fulfil some EU quota. Every now and then the commentators would present statistics which would show that the forward had a strike-rate of one goal every four games, which they assured us was quite reasonable.

It all looked quite miserable: that one moment of scoring euphoria was hardly compensation for six otherwise bleak hours spent with your back to goal. But, I'll admit, watching such a dull spectacle made me feel a guilty smugness, the same quiet satisfaction you felt when you drove through a soulless satellite town and thanked whatever God you worshipped that you didn't live there. This, after all, was Italian football; and its negative ways would never infect the Premier League, my Premier League, which was the last remaining bastion of tactical abandon and defensive irresponsibility in Europe.

Not so, said Opta's Duncan Alexander. He told me that English football had been drifting towards Italian football for longer than I'd realised. The three lowest-scoring seasons since the Premier League began in 1992 had all occurred since 2005. The highest goal-per-game average had come in 1999–2000, at 2.79 goals per game; by 2006–07, that was down to 2.45. It also seemed that a familiar pantomime villain was partially to blame: "It was quite noticeable that in '04–'05, when Mourinho came in [to Chelsea], there was a significant drop in goals per game… since '04, the lone striker has become a lot more prevalent." Further, Alexander pointed out that neither Steven Gerrard nor Cristiano Ronaldo, who at the time were leading the league in scoring, were traditional strikers.

The message was clear enough: those lonely forwards I saw in Serie A had now migrated to the UK. It wasn't the primary job of the striker to score any more, but rather to create room for the onrushing midfielders. The days of two specialist centre-forwards, who barely left the penalty area and certainly wouldn't come back to mark at corners, were long gone. If you were a tactical traditionalist, the sort who, if your house was burning down, would dial 442 as the emergency number, then this was very bad news.

"Keep your shape"

On the bright side, there was good news for the followers of Sun Tzu's teachings; his insistence upon disciplined deployment of troops, on rigid retention of tactical shape, was to be found alive and flourishing in the colours of Roy Hodgson's Fulham FC. Sun Tzu wrote that "one defends when his strength is inadequate; he attacks when it is abundant". Hodgson, who'd been appointed as Fulham manager in December 2007, was a firm adherent to this view – he wasn't doing much attacking at all, and for good reason. His team, inherited from the hapless Lawrie Sanchez, had gone a record thirty-three games without an away win, but had still somehow escaped relegation: I quickly found out why.

In early 2009, I went to watch his team twice within a week; first away to Arsenal, where they drew 0–0, and then four days later at home to Hull City, where they lost 1–0 in front of a visibly sickened Craven Cottage crowd. What I saw during those three largely goalless hours was a team that was coached as impressively as any that I'd witnessed. As you can see from those two results, Fulham didn't score many goals. But they didn't concede many either. At the time I'd gone to see them, they'd proudly established the fourth finest defensive record in the Premier League, behind only Manchester

United, Chelsea and Liverpool; a defence, moreover, that they'd put together at a fraction of what these other three teams had spent.

Fulham, of course, would use this excellent defensive foundation as a basis for spectacular success in the coming season, reaching the final of the Europa Cup – the club's first European final – defeating Juventus, Wolfsburg, Hamburg and Shaktar Donetsk along the way. It's important to note that Fulham's defence, like those of their more-vaunted rivals, didn't just comprise their back four. When anyone refers to a defence, we normally think immediately of a unit comprising five or six players; two full-backs, two centre-backs and a goal-keeper, and if you'd like a little more insurance, a defensive midfielder to screen them. However, the trend has increasingly been for managers to arrange their teams with an extra defensive midfielder; in other words, with a team containing seven defenders.

What's more, a defensive player of the highest class can cost almost as much as an exceptional centre-forward. Brian Clough once wondered why goalkeepers didn't cost as much as strikers, given that a great save was often worth as much as a great goal; he would have smiled, then, to see Gianluigi Buffon move from Parma to Juventus for £32 million in 2001. Moreover, the summer after Fernando Torres moved from Atlético Madrid to Liverpool for £20.2 million, Manchester United spent an initial £14 million, rising to £18.6 million, to take Michael Carrick from Tottenham Hotspur, and a further undisclosed sum, believed to be in the region of £17 million, on Owen Hargreaves; a combined sum of over £35 million for two midfield anchormen.

Money often tells the truest tale in football, and in that sense the Carrick transfer represented a passing of the tactical torch. Michael Owen had moved from Real Madrid to Newcastle, costing the Tyneside club some £16 million;

twelve months later, he would see Carrick go to Old Trafford for roughly the same amount, Carrick, who despite his apparently casual demeanour, made more tackles than anyone in the Premier League. Arguably the final step in this tactical sea-change was the acknowledgement of Barcelona and Spain's Xavi – a true disciple of Rinus Michels' "circulation football" – as the player of the UEFA 2008 tournament. In previous years, the award might have gone to David Villa, Spain's top goal scorer during their triumph; but since then there had been a recognition of the role of the players who conduct attacking operations from the base of midfield.

Counter-attack was all the rage in Sun Tzu's day; it's taken football a few thousand years to catch up, but now the game values defence as highly as attack, if not more so. So I suppose, in conclusion, that we should thank Sun Tzu for his *Art of War*. At this point, you might wish him to rest in peace; but then again, peace probably wasn't his thing.

CASE STUDY 2, STRATEGY

THE TAO OF HENRY GREGG

How to win a Fantasy Football League title

I wonder, if Sun Tzu were alive today, how good he would have been at Fantasy League Football. Most importantly, I wonder if he would have been as good as Henry Gregg. Gregg, as we saw in the chapter on Obsession, won the Fantasyleague.com title in the 2005–06 season; and he did so with an attention to detail that would have made the Chinese strategist proud.

Knowing that there would be countless people interested in the secrets of his success, I plied Gregg with a pint or two of ale so that he might dispense this essential wisdom. He kindly obliged, as a result of which we can exclusively present *The Tao of Henry Gregg: The Guide To Winning a Fantasy League Title*.

Lesson one: the team name

Every glory-seeking fantasy league team must start with a notable name; some contestants choose names of personal significance, whilst others go for playful puns. Gregg went for the latter. In homage to both the then Arsenal winger Alexsandr Hleb, and a famous Beatles anthem, he called his side "Hleb, I Need Somebody". Whilst a season-ticket holder at Arsenal – he gave up his ticket in disgust at Arsène Wenger's reluctance to buy experienced players – he had tried to begin a chant of "Hleb, I Need Somebody" among his fellow fans. His attempt had failed. "The thing is," he mused, "when you try to start a song like that, you're pretty much on your own."

Lesson two: buy cheap in defence and midfield

"Don't spend big money on midfielders, for a start," said Gregg, "and, whatever you do, don't buy defensive midfielders. Work out who the regular back four is, week in, week out, of any team, and then choose the cheapest defender of that back four. Say the usual left-back for Chelsea has been injured; Ashley Cole has been injured for four months, so you bring in Zhirkov, because you know he's going to play there, and he's going to be cheap, because at the start of the season [your rival managers] will all have thought, 'Well, Zhirkov's going to be on the bench, Ashley Cole's going to play every game, therefore [Yuri] Zhirkov's going to be a lot cheaper.'"

Lesson three: spend big in attack, and take a risk

"Get one striker who scores goals and assists [such as Thierry Henry], and then, make a punt on a striker," advised Gregg. "I punted on [Charlton Athletic's] Darren Bent at the start of the season, and obviously that was his breakout season. There's always one player who comes up with a promoted team and scores a ton of goals – remember [Ipswich Town's] Marcus Stewart, a few years ago? Have one instrumental striker, and one cheap striker."

Lesson four: desperately seeking set-pieces

"Find out who takes the corners and free-kicks for each team. That's a really, really big thing. If you look at a team like Bolton or Blackburn, they're going to get a lot of goals from corners and free-kicks. So [Morten Gamst] Pedersen, for example, who was at Blackburn at that time, was taking all their free-kicks and headers; and although he wasn't scoring that many goals, he was the one who was putting it on the heads of all these bruisers who were knocking it in the back of the net. If you go to the BBC [website] for the live text commentaries on football matches, it tells you who takes the corners and free-kicks."

Lesson five: be lucky

In a league of 60,000 competitors, the margin for error is infinitesimal; accordingly, there's nothing that will serve you better in the final weeks of the season than a great deal of fortune. Every now and then, a player will have an unprecedented run of brilliant form which will prove decisive in the division. In 2005–06, that man was Thierry Henry; out for most of the year with injury, he returned to full fitness in the last few crucial games. What was more, Gregg was the only person near the top of the fantasy league table with Henry in his team; no one else could afford him by then.

"[Henry] absolutely tore the league apart," recalled Gregg. "He scored a hat-trick in his last game against Wigan, but before that he scored a couple of goals against Sunderland, and he was getting assists all over the place. I was just shooting up the league. On the last day of the season I was still ten points behind this player... and Henry scored a hat-trick, which meant that Arsenal got fourth [place in the Premier League, therefore qualifying for the UEFA Champions League], Tottenham lost, and I won the fantasy league. So it was a perfect day for me... It also was Arsenal's last match at Highbury."

Lesson six: no plan is fail-safe

No matter how well you apply the previous five principles, which are all undeniably excellent, there will always be an obstacle to your Fantasy League success. For Gregg, it came in a familiar but no less devastating form. "My girlfriend said, 'You're spending too much time on the fantasy league,'" he said wistfully, "and she made a rule that I don't play it in the house."

COMMUNICATION

Managers must communicate well. Whether they're using words, hands, flying objects or even birds of prey (bear with me; all will become clear), they must get their points across effectively to their players, directors, rivals or whoever else could be vital or fatal to their chances of success. When people think of a manager communicating, one of the first images that springs to mind is normally that of a gaffer, foaming with fury at his team's first-half performance, bellowing at each of his players as they cower in the dressing-room. It's often said that "a manager earns his money at half-time"; that only the very top managers can produce the inspired advice that can turn around matches their teams are losing. There's truth in that, but not the whole truth; you'll need to have much, much more than a cuss-littered team-talk in your locker to be any good at this job. The art of communication is the art of setting the tone, and the very best do this without saying a single word.

The truth is in the team-sheet

To learn a person's fate, some people read tea-leaves. In football, we read the manager's team-sheet. It's his statement of intent, a frank admission of who he's playing and how he's playing them. For a loyal supporter, looking at the team-sheet for the first time is a little like drawing back your curtains in the morning to take your first tentative look at the day: what you see there will make your spirit either sink or soar.

Italian moods took a sudden plummet when Azeglio Vicini, the national team's manager at the 1990 World Cup, revealed his lineup for the semi-final against Argentina. The selection the country clamoured for was that of Roberto Baggio, who in a previous round had scored what would prove to be the goal of the tournament, a 2–0 victory over Czechoslovakia. But, among the surnames of those players confirmed to start, Baggio was nowhere to be seen. He was instead a substitute, Vicini having decided to pick Gianluca Vialli, who had returned from injury. In making this decision, Vicini showed himself to be a conservative, choosing in Vialli a forward of established pedigree, as opposed to one whose profile was rising with alarming rapidity. Perhaps Vicini also showed that he was afraid to dream.

Archbishop Desmond Tutu, speaking in a different context, once said that "our deepest fear is not that we are inadequate. It is that we are powerful beyond measure." Tutu thought that what really made us freeze when presented with a great challenge wasn't the challenge itself; it was the thought that we, little old we, would be able to surmount it with ease. I wonder whether, on the eve of a World Cup semi-final hosted by his own country, against the defending world champions, Vicini looked Fate in the face, and then looked away. Maybe he was scared to unleash Baggio against Diego Maradona, to let his team's talisman confront the South American legend right from the very start. His reason for not doing so was somewhat unconvincing. On the morning of the match, Vicini had taken Baggio to one side and informed him that he would begin on the bench. Baggio's reaction, like that of his nation, was one of disbelief. "He said I looked tired," he would later divulge. "I was only twenty-three! I would have eaten grass to play."

Without wishing to distract you from the discussion of whether or not Vicini lost his nerve, it's worth observing that Baggio thought there could be no greater sacrifice for one's country than a spot of gentle grazing. Now, whilst we don't know why Baggio held grass in such low esteem, we do know that Vicini brought him on as a substitute in the second-half against Argentina, and that Baggio was sufficiently firm of resolve to score in the ensuing penalty shoot-out (which Italy lost). So Baggio can't have been that much in need of a rest; and by the time he came onto the pitch, the die had been cast. Argentina knew that Italy would rather wrap their greatest weapon in cotton wool than wield him, and – though a shadow of the team they had been in 1986 – they made their way through to the final.

By contrast, a manager not noted for his sense of adventure once sent the strongest of all messages with his team-sheet. Throughout his time in charge of England Sven-Göran Eriksson was criticised, not without foundation, for both his tactical timidity and deference to senior players. Against Brazil in the quarter-final of the 2002 World Cup, losing by 2–1 but with an extra man after the dismissal of Ronaldinho, he failed to force the initiative, allowing the opposition effectively to keep the ball for the last half-hour of the match, and to prevail by a single goal. Though this was excruciating viewing, it takes only second place in the symbolic moments of Eriksson's England tenure.

First place must go to the selection of David Beckham, the then captain, as a deep-lying playmaker, in the mould of Andrea Pirlo, against Northern Ireland in a World Cup qualifier in September 2005. Beckham was deployed in what infamously became known as the "quarterback" role in a 4–5–1 formation; he was positioned slightly south of Frank Lampard and Steven Gerrard in central midfield. The idea was that from this vantage point he could loft long and languid passes to the right flank and to the left flank, to where Wayne Rooney had been shifted to accommodate him.

Beckham himself played well, but those around him did not; England's subsequent 1–0 loss to the home side was their first defeat in Belfast since 1927. There was persistent rumour that Eriksson was unduly influenced by his captain, and *The Onion Bag*, a football satire website, duly carried a particularly ruthless spoof of his strategy. In a mock interview, Eriksson was quoted as saying, "At first I thought it was a bad idea. But Dave sat down with me and explained how the new system works. One or two players will have to play out of position and we may lose some matches but as long as Dave's happy that is all that matters."

There was vehement denial from Eriksson that he had been even remotely swayed by Beckham's wishes; and, indeed, the bravest decision that the Swede took whilst England manager speaks volumes for his character. Eriksson's team was due to play Turkey in a qualifying match for the 2004 European Championships; the group was close, following a run of indifferent form by England, and there was one seventeen-year-old whom everyone (except, perhaps, Turkey) wanted to see on the team-sheet.

Everton's Wayne Rooney, like Roberto Baggio thirteen years before him, had cast himself into the nation's consciousness with a goal of sublime quality. Arsenal, who had been unbeaten for thirty league matches, had come to Goodison Park, never the easiest place to win at; they looked like they'd be leaving with a point, the game tied at 1–1 in injury time, until Rooney stepped in. Bringing a high ball under control, he looked up and then rifled a swerving drive that bruised the crossbar on its way in.

Rooney's subsequent form has proved that goal to be no fluke; he'd previously starred as a substitute, and so Eriksson gave him his full debut against Turkey. In an accomplished 2–0 victory, Rooney was man of the match, rewarding Eriksson for daring to go where Vicini didn't. The cynics might argue that he was persuaded by his players, who publicly called for Rooney's selection; or that he was persuaded by the media, particularly by a tabloid survey which showed that 70 per cent of its readers thought Rooney should play. But ultimately, as we'll see in the chapter on Resilience, it's the manager who lives and dies by the decisions that he makes; and, for his willingness to strike a defiantly attacking note, Eriksson should be applauded.

Cracking down

Another wordless way of setting the tone is money; or, in particular, docking players their wages for ill-discipline. Duncan Alexander of Opta Sports, who was a Wycombe Wanderers supporter, recalled the hard line taken by one of his team's former managers. "I remember when John Gregory was there," Alexander told me. "I don't know why, but he had a hatred of players shooting from long-range. He used to fine players if they shot from outside the box. I remember once we beat Bristol Rovers 4–3 and all four goals were long-range… it was joked that it was going to cost the players two hundred quid for winning the game!"

Less bizarrely, Brent Hills, the assistant head coach of the England Women's team, told me of a training course that he'd once attended with Rinus Michels, where the great Dutchman was asked how he'd imposed his authority on a Holland dressing-room, including enormous egos such as those of Johann Cruyff and Ruud Krol. Michels replied that he'd simply said, on the first day, that he wouldn't tolerate lateness for training, and anyone who didn't arrive on time would be fined two weeks' pay. Krol duly arrived fifteen minutes late; Michels duly fined him as promised; and no one was late after that. More recently, FC Barcelona's Pep Guardiola has taken the same approach. On arriving at the Nou Camp in 2008, he swept away some of the vestiges of Frank Rijkaard's supposedly slack regime by imposing fines for different transgressions; 500 euros for missing breakfast with the squad, and 6,000 euros for lateness.

Some might argue that merely giving financial penalties to players is only of symbolic significance, given the vast sums they earn. They might be right: Hills pointed out that if you took two week's wages from one of today's male top-flight players, he'd barely notice. Manchester City's Mark Hughes found himself in that predicament: in 2009, when Robinho walked out on a training camp in Tenerife, Hughes fined the former Real Madrid star an eye-watering £320,000. However, this didn't result in a string of outstanding performances from the Brazilian.

Rules are another means of setting the tone before you've barely spoken a word to your players. Real Madrid literally lays down the law to its new signings, issuing each of them with a book on their arrival which details how they should conduct themselves as representatives of the club. Many managers have become well-known for what they will and will not tolerate, and when Fabio Capello stepped into the role of England manager, it seemed that a thorough realignment of priorities was needed. Much has been made in preceding years of the negative effect of WAGs – that is to say, the proliferation of glamorous wives and girlfriends who would distract the England players during international tournaments, with their well-publicised nights out on the town. Before Rio Ferdinand spoke on the matter prior to a World Cup 2008 qualifier against Belarus, no England player had been quite so honest about the need for root-and-branch reform.

"I think we got caught up in all the hype," confessed Ferdinand, discussing England's preparations under manager

Sven-Göran Eriksson for the 2006 World Cup in Germany. "We became celebrities in terms of the WAG situation. There was a big show around the England squad. It was like a theatre unfolding, and football became a secondary element to the main event. People were worrying more about what people were wearing and where we were going, rather than the England football team. We were caught in the bubble ourselves... walking around, there were paparazzi everywhere, our families were there. When you step back it was like a circus."

Sex, plus food

Ferdinand spoke of a "show", "theatre" and "circus", which the public might not have minded so much had England provided a carnival on the pitch: but they didn't. Their departure from the World Cup on penalties, following a goalless draw against Portugal, left the mood ripe for a crackdown which, following the dismissal of Steve McClaren two years later, belatedly arrived. Fabio Capello came into his role as England manager with a satisfyingly draconian list of demands. "The Italian rules with an iron fist," reported the *Mirror*'s Steve Stammers, somewhat breathlessly, in April 2009. A litany of strictures followed: Capello would not use nicknames when addressing his players, and he also insisted upon "punctuality, a dress code, a ban on mobile phones at meal times and a new schedule ahead of training". Elsewhere, *The Times* solemnly reported that family members, friends and agents had been banned from the team hotel.

My own favourite Capello directive, though, emerged when the Italian reflected on the type of partner that England players could conceivably invite to see them at training camps – and the type they could not. "When I was a club manager," recalled Capello, "then sometimes during long training camps – ten or fifteen days – it was possible to meet the women, the wives or the official girlfriends. Not strange girlfriends."

Regrettably, Capello didn't elaborate on what he meant by "strange girlfriends". Helpfully, however, the Italian forward Antonio Cassano, who played under Capello at Roma and Real Madrid, provided a useful indicator. Whilst at Real Madrid Cassano, who claimed to have bedded between 600 and 700 women, made the acquaintance of a waiter at a hotel who would regularly smuggle girls up the back stairs for him. These women only ever stayed for one night, so it's probable they would have qualified as "strange girlfriends" under Capello's guidelines.

Cassano, for what it's worth, seemed more preoccupied with another type of present that the waiter would bring him of an evening. In his autobiography *Dico Tutto (I'll Tell Everything)*, he wrote that the waiter's job was "to bring me three or four *cornetti* (an Italian pastry) after I had sex. He would bring the *cornetti* to the stairs, I would bring the girl and we would make a trade: he took the girl, I stuffed myself with *cornetti*. Sex plus food, the perfect night."

Playing the media

When dealing with footballers as unruly as Cassano, managers will frequently turn to the media as an ally. "The media" at first seems a broad, nebulous term. After all, the media consists of so many different elements that it's impossible to describe them all in one breath. The media comprises everyone who publishes any kind of view on football; the raw-red-meat-chewing tabloid columnists, the penny-loafered television pundits, the haughty or broadsheet intellectuals with their BBC Radio brogues; the wide-eyed, hyperactive newscasters, the old-school commentators, who are half-orator, half-scholar... and then there are the bloggers: not hundreds of blogs but thousands of them, whose authors, mostly anonymous, subject the game's major and minor figures to constant, and often caustic, analysis.

Yet the media does follow basic rules, which the best managers are all too happy to exploit. The most important of these is that it adopts a herd mentality; if a major story or theme is carried with success by one media outlet, then most if not all the others will follow suit, however begrudgingly. The media, after all, is a business, and – other than the free-spirited bloggers, who have overwhelmingly been a force for good in the game – competing organisations would rather be conservative and cover the same ground as each other rather than ignore the popular stories and thus concede market share.

And so, if a manager makes a cleverly controversial statement, then he'll rest assured in the knowledge that it will be repeated *ad nauseam* across the full range of papers on his breakfast table. As a Manchester United fan, the best piece of player manipulation via the media that I'd seen from Sir Alex Ferguson came in September 2007. That summer, the club had signed Anderson, a Brazilian midfielder, from FC Porto for £17 million; a sum showing their faith that he'd make a significant, if not instant impact. Unfortunately, the first time that Anderson would grace the news pages would be when the tabloids reported that one weekend he, along with teammates Nani and Cristiano Ronaldo, had hired some escorts for a private party.

Ferguson's public response was delayed, but decisive. A few weeks later, following a 2–0 defeat to Coventry in the Carling Cup, the Scotsman struck, in the form of a comment that casually leaked its way out of the Manchester United dressing room. Daniel Taylor, the *Guardian*'s reporter at Old Trafford, wrote that Anderson was "facing a prolonged spell in the reserves after an unflattering start to life with his new club. It has been made clear to Ferguson," continued Taylor, "that the teenager may need a longer bedding-in period than had initially been anticipated. Ferguson has told his colleagues it may be a year before the player, a full Brazil international, is ready to seriously challenge for a first-team place, an astonishing admission given the amount of money it took to sign him from Porto."

Within a few months of the emergence of this story, Anderson was excelling in an unfamiliar position in defensive midfield; he was signed as a playmaker, expected to weave elegant spells just off the shoulder of his centre-forward, but was soon acquitting himself to fine effect, most remarkably against Liverpool's Steven Gerrard. We can deduce, then, that Ferguson was probably being mischievous when he told his colleagues that it would be a year before Anderson could seriously challenge for a first-team place. There's often nothing like applying public stings to footballers' pride to get them moving on the pitch, and so it proved with the Brazilian who, when fit, became a first-team regular.

Ferguson's approach to the Anderson affair had been somewhat cloak-and-dagger; those who prefer a full-frontal philosophy to attacking one's footballers would prefer the methods of Giovanni Trappatoni. In a March 1998 press conference, Trappatoni, then manager of Bayern Munich, tore into those of his playing staff who he felt were taking him for a ride. The conference was a triumph of anger over grammar; though his relationship with the German language was still a fledgling one, Trappatoni raged with a passion that was unambiguous, hammering away at the rostrum with his hands as if it were the head of an overpaid prima donna. "A coach, not an idiot!" he roared. "And these players… these players were weak like a bottle empty!"

The performance, visible of course on YouTube, is different depending on your vantage point; whilst it's amusing to the rest of the world, it would have been unsettling if not terrifying were you its direct target – like Thomas Strunz, Bayern's perennially crocked defensive midfielder. "Strunz!" yelled Trappatoni. "Strunz is two years here, has played ten game! Is always injured. What dare Strunz?" Having thus dispatched his chief bugbear, the Italian then professed that he was thoroughly sick of it all. "I am tired now the father these players and defend these players," he said. "I have always the blame. Over these players." Unsurprisingly – given that Bayern Munich is nicknamed FC Hollywood, due to the drama that always seems to surround the club both on and off the pitch – Trappatoni was gone at the end of the season.

Despite his untimely departure from Bayern, Trappatoni's communication skills generally stood him in good stead throughout his career: he remains the only manager to have won all of the UEFA club competitions, a feat which he achieved with Juventus. (Perhaps we make too much of the fact that, in the modern era of globalised football, a manager must be multilingual in order for his team to receive his instructions; we're ignoring good old-fashioned player chemistry. At Parma in the mid-1990s, Gianfranco Zola played alongside Faustino Asprilla and formed a spectacular partnership with the Colombian, a relationship unhindered by the fact that they shared few words in common. "Me and Asprilla? We never talked to each other!" Zola told me, laughing. "We couldn't talk! No, with me and Asprilla it wasn't talking, it was understanding. Just pure understanding. I knew what he wanted from me, I knew what I wanted from him, and it just worked… And it was the same with Careca, Maradona, you know? You didn't need to speak, you didn't need to tell him 'I'm going to go there, you pass me the ball there.' No! You'll come together; because when football brains meet, you don't need words."

A brief lesson in mindgames

Of course, Trappatoni wasn't alone when it came to using press conferences for dramatic effect. Another manager famed for doing so was Liverpool's Rafa Benítez, whose broadside against Sir Alex Ferguson during the 2008–09 Premier League season was widely regarded as a turning-point in that year's title race, shifting the momentum irresistibly towards Manchester United. Ferguson's team would go on to win the championship by just two points, and Benítez was to blame. Although I disagreed with this view, the episode said much about the workings of the media, and the degree of control that his bitter rival exerted over it.

At a press conference on 9 January 2009, Rafa Benítez took out a piece of paper and read from it a series of carefully-prepared comments; he was concerned to address the extent to which, in his view, personnel at Manchester United unfairly influenced the decisions made by match officials. Benítez spoke in a tone that was more level than livid; but, by the time the story reached the news wire, his speech had become a "rant". In fairness, the *Penguin Dictionary* does define a rant as "to talk in a noisy, excited or *declamatory* manner" (my italics), which Benítez just about did, but this did seem to be stretching it a little. The papers, inevitably, would go further. According to the *Guardian*, Benítez "erupted". The *Mirror* called it an "amazing blast". Benítez was "barmy" in the *Daily Mail*, and it was left to Sir Alex Ferguson of all people to remain more temperate than most, simply describing the Spaniard's comments as "weird".

In trying to wind up Benítez, Ferguson may have followed the advice of the Chinese scholar Chang Yü, who counselled that "if the enemy general is obstinate and prone to anger, insult and enrage him, so that he will be irritated and confused, and without a plan will recklessly advance against you". Then again, this was not the first time Ferguson had been involved in a mind-game with a fellow leading manager.

Much has been made of the success of these mind games, but I wondered how effective they truly were or are. Most neutrals will recall the famous occasion, when pursuing the league championship in 1997, that Ferguson questioned the commitment of Leeds United, who were due to play against Kevin Keegan's Newcastle United side. Newcastle, United's closest rivals that year, had at one period led them by twelve points, but were beginning to exhibit an alarming frailty under pressure. Ferguson's innuendo accordingly met with long shrift from Keegan.

Clearly distressed, Keegan gave a live BBC interview in which, with raised voice and jabbed finger, he roared that he would love it, love it, if United lost the title; but as Keegan lost his self-control, so Newcastle lost their way, finishing second in the table. However, there are several other occasions on which Ferguson has applied his sting, only to receive far sharper barbs. The most prominent of these was probably when, in 2002, he fumed that despite Arsenal being ahead of United in the league table, it was his team, not Wenger's, that was playing the more attractive football. Wenger's return of serve was as magnificent as that of Roger Federer. "Everyone," he replied, "thinks they have the prettiest wife at home."

However, speaking with Guillem Balague, a leading football journalist and analyst with Sky Sports, he was adamant that these duels had little effect on players. Meanwhile Gabriele Marcotti, of *The Times*, saw Benítez's supposed rant not as a loss of cool in the face of Ferguson's provocation, but as a speech which had "broader objectives". He thought that the Liverpool manager was aiming to make newspapers stop and think about the referees who were consistently being lenient towards Manchester United: "to get a little campaign going, and what that would have done is, the next time a referee officiates Manchester United, then he will have it at the back of his mind that maybe he won't give the big club the benefit of the doubt."

Benítez, as Marcotti dryly noted, hadn't succeeded on this occasion, mainly because the media decided that he was crazy and ran with that narrative instead. To be fair to Benítez, though, there was another occasion, during his days in charge of Valencia, on which he played the press to perfection, and which it's worth highlighting here. In *Rafa Benítez*, Paco Lloret's biography of the Spaniard, the following scene takes place at Valencia's stadium:

"The League is still possible." That was Benítez's message to a small group of journalists gathered for an impromptu midnight meeting at the Mestalla premises. There were no microphones. No one took any notes. The manager had conducted his press conference with no assumptions about the future, nor had there been any smugness. He was now spilling the beans in an informal meeting.

If we're looking at just how skilfully Benítez has courted the media in his time, then there are a few things worth noting from the above paragraph. The first is the size of the gathering: a small group, so that each member in attendance will feel as if they've passed some sort of secret test of integrity, of allegiance, or both. The chances are that they'll have looked around curiously on arrival, their relief at having been invited swiftly replaced by glee at those who've not been similarly chosen.

The second thing to note is the time of the gathering. Midnight, under the cover of darkness; it's a theatrical gesture, and shows that Benítez, like all other great managers, is something of a drama queen. What's more, it's a power move. The journalists then present will have wives, or deadlines, significant others, all of which might require their attention in the dead of night. But, instead, they're here; at the beck and call of Benítez.

Finally, there's the control. Not only is Benítez controlling his message's content, context and the composition of its captive audience; he's also controlling how the message is being absorbed. No notes, no microphones. The journalists will have to run home to their notebooks or laptops, the only evidence of his thoughts being the echo of his wise words in their ears. Benítez is now literally in their heads; he's given them no other way to receive him. What's more, since they've not been able to take a single thing down, the journalists will have to use their imaginations to evoke the tone that Benítez used. And, because most memories are imperfect stores, they'll all remember his words, and the intensity with which they were delivered, slightly differently.

Some will recall the manager's tone as casual; others as conspiratorial. One of them will go home and write: "Rafa insists: 'The League is still possible.'" Another will say: "'Game on,' barks Benítez." And one, who's particularly excitable – there's always one – will write: "Rafa: 'Madrid: We're Coming For You'." What Benítez had created was a grateful, attentive – and, therefore, possibly pliable – group of messengers for his cause. We must remember that most communication is non-verbal; and so, whilst Benítez told them that "the League is still possible", his real message was: "Be thankful. I have brought you into my innermost world. You are here at my time, on my terms." Now, that's as good an example as any of how to engage the press. But I've looked elsewhere for a fine demonstration of another one of the manager's essential arts; and that's the team talk.

The art of the team talk

Just before I passed my twelfth birthday, I heard what was

probably the greatest team talk in the world. I was shortly to play in my debut for Sunningdale, a prep school that I attended just outside Ascot; the match, the first of the season, was against our enduring rivals, Ludgrove. Ludgrove was more or less a small, family business, founded in the late nineteenth century, its reasonably strict governance based upon core Judeo-Christian principles; as your car rolled into its grounds, your spirits eased, entering as you were what seemed the dreamiest of country retreats, sitting tranquilly near the Surrey borders. In other words, Ludgrove were exactly like us, and therefore we hated them.

Hate, I hasten to add, wasn't something we were taught at school; it was something we young footballers learned from painful experience. It wasn't really Ludgrove's fault: it's just that if you beat them at anything, it was something you remembered years later, and if you lost to them at anything, well, it was something you remembered years later.

It's years later now and I can still feel the school minibus rattling towards that first real confrontation of my prepubescent football career, towards this Rome derby of the stockbroker belt. The slick sheen of my new tracksuit top, my nostrils watering from the Arctic sharpness of that Deep Heat ointment I'd massaged into my thighs; and our magnificent football kit. Shirts and socks in shimmering pale blue, set against dark blue shorts; it was strange as a Manchester United fan to be so much in love with Manchester City's colours, but that was far from the last time the game of football would surprise me.

So I looked the part; but I didn't feel it, and neither did my team-mates. There's a scene near the start of James Cameron's *Aliens*, where a spacecraft brings a squadron of Marines shuddering down through the atmosphere of a distant, foreign world, each jolt that the ship takes towards its destination sending fresh trepidation through its passengers. We were travelling a shorter distance than those GIs – Ludgrove was only eleven miles from Sunningdale – and were on our way to do battle with slightly less hostile creatures, but we were probably similarly worried.

Our team wasn't short of talkers: there, you'd have our right-back trying to deadpan you into believing some typically ridiculous urban myth, and here, you'd have our number 10 dredging up some obscure sporting statistic from the last century, and, as the new boy, I'd be throwing in the odd sly comment at the team's veterans (all of thirteen years old) and seeing how much cheek I could usefully get away with. But as we drew close to Ludgrove, this chatter swiftly fell away, and the bus grew hollow with silence.

Nick Dawson, one of our two headmasters – he ran the school with his twin brother, Tim – was our driver that day, and most importantly our manager. Slender, silver-haired and flat-capped, he'd been a leading schools sprinter in his youth, and some decades on he retained that quickness elsewhere, in his wit. As he turned off the A-road to make the final approach, he looked into his rear-view mirror, and saw thirteen faces full of fear. So he smiled, and said to us something simple and brilliant: "You're going to play for an hour; that's sixty minutes. There will be twenty-two of you on the pitch. Each of you will probably have the ball for no more than two minutes at most: maybe no more than ten or fifteen touches. Make them count."

That's all he said; and somehow that scorching September afternoon seemed immediately softer. Moods lightened, chatter returned, and the boots on my feet felt less like clogs. We sauntered out onto that sun-seared pitch in front of 300 pupils and parents, and won 1–0 with a very, very late goal.

Looking back, it's as much what he didn't say, as what he did; if you're preparing your team for a great campaign, it's best to keep things short. It distracts them from the scale of the task ahead, and gives them a sense of high urgency but low pressure.

Nick Dawson's approach was sanguine, but anger can still be highly effective. Tales abound, for example, of Sir Alex Ferguson's "hairdryer treatment", which consists of a sustained blast of Glaswegian rage only a few inches from the guilty players' faces; this is a perception that Ferguson himself has done little to dispel. Here, after all, is a paragraph from *Managing My Life*, his autobiography, in which he describes a confrontation with one of his players, the Aberdeen and Scotland midfielder Gordon Strachan:

> The wee man was, however, in one of his nippy sweetie moods, full of caustic comments. What he regarded as smart ripostes struck me as senseless meanderings and as I intensified my onslaught I swung a hand in anger at a huge tea urn that was nearby. It was made of pewter or iron and striking it nearly broke my hand. The pain caused me to flip my lid and I hurled a tray of cups filled with tea towards Strachan, hitting the wall above him.

Unsurprisingly, noted Ferguson, "Strachan obeyed orders in the second half."

Yet Paul Simpson, the editor of *Champions* (the official magazine for the UEFA Champions League), pointed out that Ferguson's approach could be far more measured than that. He reminded me of September 2001, when Manchester United had beaten Tottenham 5–3 at White Hart Lane, having been 0–3 down at half-time. It was widely thought at the time that United's remarkable renaissance was due to Ferguson scaring the life out of them. Ferguson himself seemed happy for this perception to continue, hinting to the media that he'd played the ogre. "I'm not saying exactly what I said to the players at half-time," said Ferguson, "but the essence of it was to stop feeling sorry for themselves. These are the best players in the country and they should play like that."

Simpson told a different tale. "My publisher was up at Old Trafford, and he asked Denis Irwin [former full-back] what Ferguson said to them at half-time. He said, 'Ferguson didn't use the hairdryer. What he said, very calmly, was, "Obviously, you know that this is Spurs we're playing. In their minds, they've already won, they're in the pub after the game celebrating. Get a goal back at the beginning of the second half and they'll panic. That's the thing about Spurs. They've always played like that, and they always will."'"

Whips and eagles

In order to make their points more forcefully, managers may resort to the use of visual aids. Tea cups did the trick for Ferguson, but others have turned to more exotic means. Eberhard Spohd, in a submission to Paul Doyle's column in the *Guardian*, related the tale of Klaus Toppmöller; who, when he "was attempting to win the title with Eintracht Frankfurt, showed the players a replica of the Meisterschale, the big, ugly plate the German champion gets for coming in first". Having failed to rouse his charges, "He tried with a huge living eagle (the animal in the coat of arms of Eintracht) which he brought into the changing room with the words: 'You must clutch your opposites like the eagle puts his fangs in his prey.' The order was clear enough, but as Doyle reveals, it didn't have the desired effect. "The players seemed rather scared and finished fifth, and Toppmöller was sacked the following April."

Urging your players to claw at the other team like feral predators is unlikely to work. Neither is threatening them with mortal peril. Uday, the deceased son of the Iraqi dictator Saddam Hussein, was during the eighties the main influence behind the national side, and his incentives to perform were notoriously vicious. As *Soccerlens.com* informs us, "Failure was not an option, and as a result, any sign of weakness in the players wearing the national shirt resulted in torture, humiliation and severe punishment." The article continues:

> Stories have emerged in the aftermath of the death of Uday and the falling of the prior regime about how players who missed good chances in matches would be imprisoned for up to a month for their crimes. How missing a training session because of a family illness or death meant repeated flogging with electric cable and how *a missed penalty in a shoot-out* would result in players being forced to take baths in vats of raw sewage. (My italics.)

There's not really much that you can say, except that it's strange that dictators or their psychotic offspring should choose to pin their prestige on a sport as fickle as football. From one angle, I understand the logic of it; that football is the most widely-watched sport in the world, and if the country succeeds at football, then the dictator or the psychotic offspring is seen to be a tremendous success, thereby legitimising the regime. Well-oiled rumours of his savagery will evaporate on the winds once he's seen clutching the trophy in a hastily arranged photo opportunity; if, say, North Korea win an Asian football title, everyone will forget that their ruler has an itchy nuclear trigger finger. So goes the theory.

But aside from its barbarism, the other problem with Uday's approach is its impossibility. One of the reasons that the Ten Commandments have been the cornerstone of Christianity for two thousand years is that they're mostly orders which, with a fair bit of self-discipline, people can *actually follow*. If you tell someone not to kill or not to steal or not to commit adultery, or not to covet his neighbour's wife, these are things that he can bring himself to do. They're well within his physical and emotional remit. However, any religion whose first commandment is "Thou shalt not miss a penalty in a shoot-out" would be doomed to failure. Other than Chelsea's Michael Ballack and the former Manchester United full-back Denis Irwin – whom I'd never seen miss penalties, and if they have they've kept it very quiet – such a religion would have no members. If every man who bottled it from the spot was damned, Hell would be a populous place indeed.

Communication as storytelling: show, don't tell

It's important, then, to give your players instructions that they're able to follow; this, again, was where Aidy Boothroyd stood out. The training sessions that he ran with the England Writers team were broken into segments of either two minutes or four minutes; so you were never far away from either your next break, or your next crisp instruction. If a particular exercise was proving difficult to master, then it was quickly dispensed with; this was very useful for the slower-witted members of the squad, whose brains hadn't travelled as far south as their feet. For example, I was behind the sabotage of one of Boothroyd's "Ajax squares", an intricate passing pattern where you received the ball, passed it back to the person who'd passed it to you, received it again, and then passed it diagonally to someone else. It sounds simple enough now, but at the time I felt like an L-plate driver who'd just taken a turning onto a spaghetti junction. Seeing my discomfort, Boothroyd moved us swiftly on.

We had only two days' of training with him to cover six weeks' worth of training; that we absorbed so much attested to his ability, comfortably beating Norway 2–0 in our next friendly. But what was it that made him so effective? He'd mentioned that he was trained in Neuro-Linguistic Programming, or NLP, a discipline that he'd studied for over a decade, and so I thought that I'd look into it. NLP, based upon the study of the behavioural traits of successful people, aims to help people towards greater self-awareness, towards reading people better, to achieve the outcomes that you desire. The seminal work in this field, *Frogs into Princes*, was written by Richard Bandler and John Grinder, and published in 1979; helpfully, it has a trio of principles that any attentive manager should follow. Bandler and Grinder wrote:

> You need only three things to be an absolutely exquisite communicator. We have found that there are three major patterns in the behavior of every therapeutic wizard we've talked to – and executives, and salespeople. The first one is to know what outcome you want. The second is that you need flexibility in your behavior. You need to be able to generate lots of different behaviors to find out what responses you get. The third is you need to have enough sensory experience to notice when you get the responses that you want. If you have those three abilities, then you can just alter your behavior until you get the responses that you want.

Thus Boothroyd's method was made clear; each of the training exercises that we did had two purposes, the first to show us a new technique and the second to show us why that technique was of value. We weren't being drilled as robots; it was more subtle than that.

Effective communication on the training ground isn't about preaching to your players as to how they should react to every scenario they'll face on the pitch; it's about showing them precisely what all of their options are, and allowing them to decide what's best. After all, if coaching was really such a hands-on process, then the FA would allow managers to attach themselves to their players with lengths of string, and manipulate their limbs from the touchline.

Boothroyd continually pointed out that "players make decisions"; that whilst managers could instruct as much as they liked, it was ultimately the player who had the autonomy out there on the pitch. Moreover, the speed of modern football is such that, in a blink of an eye, a footballer doesn't have time to think "wait, that defender is approaching with studs raised from there; the ball is arriving here; and our striker is going to cross my path right – about – Wait, what would Rafa want me to do?" That's not how it goes; the statistic Boothroyd quoted which stood out most was that every two seconds Steven Gerrard turned his head two or three times to assess the play. That was bewildering, seeing as it was dizzy enough work to turn my head sharply two or three times in a two-second period in my own bedroom, let alone in front of 80,000 fans and midfielders who'd confiscate your ball and not give it back.

Communication with players, then, is largely an exercise in what José Mourinho has called "guided discovery", or what, say, Ernest Hemingway might call storytelling. A team's path towards success, after all, is a narrative that takes several months to unfold; and, just as the best books are the ones that you haven't been forced to read, so the best pieces of advice are those whose wisdom you've experienced for yourself. For the manager and the author alike, then, it's important to follow that age-old rule: show, don't tell.

EMPATHY

"How do I build a player up? By [first] knocking him as low as I can. I have to start from scratch with him. When I first sign a player in the pre-season and I sit with him, I spend two or three hours with him. He thinks he's coming in here just to say, 'Yeah, I'm on £150, £300 [per week],' [but] I go through everything with him. Where have you been? What have you done? You married? You got a girlfriend? You got any kids? And by the time he leaves he goes, God, I want to play for him, I love him to bits, he's great. And then I've got it into his head, that he's got to be a winner."

So spoke George Borg, a serially successful non-league manager with Braintree and Aldershot Town, on his method of moulding a player into the most effective form that he could. Manipulation is practised by all managers, and perfected only by the very best; relying, as Borg implied, on both a clinical detachment from your players, and yet an intimate understanding of their nature.

Yes: to manage your players, you won't need to love them; you won't even need to like them. They might hate you, and the feeling might be bitterly mutual. But, at all costs, you must know what makes them feel proud or frail, what makes them falter or follow you. Empathy is key. What's more, working out what type of treatment your players need, both as a group and as individuals, is a continuous process. As Eamon Dunphy wrote in *A Strange Kind of Glory*, his acclaimed biography of Manchester United legend Sir Matt Busby:

> A football club's soul is located in the dressing-room. The spirit emanating from this room will touch everyone, colour every aspect of club life. A dressing-room changes day to day, hour to hour, the mood swinging from carefree to sombre depending on all kinds of things other than results. Jealousy and resentment are harboured here, alongside pride, fulfilment and hope. Fear is also present, despair as well. Emotion is high in this unique workshop-cum-playground.

To handle those egos at any level of the game takes rare cunning; particularly at the highest level of the men's game, where the footballer has enjoyed a period of spectacular empowerment, going in just a few decades from a mere chattel of his club to a cornerstone of the entertainment industry. This evolution has been marked by a handful of major developments in contract law, a subject in which, before we look at its consequences for the modern manager, we should take a brief history lesson.

Player power

Contract law, broadly speaking, is about the balance of power between the parties to an agreement: in this case, between the player and his club. At the dawn of English football, it was clear in whose favour this relationship was weighted. Long before the existence of trade unions such as the Professional Footballers Association, or PFA, there was a registration system in place; in order to play league football, a player had to register with a particular team. So far, so good. The problem came when a player wanted to move to another club; this was summarised neatly by Dr David McArdle in his paper, "One Hundred Years of Servitude: Contractual Conflict in English Professional Football before Bosman":

If a player wanted to move clubs at the *end* of the season, he would need his old club's permission before being able to take up that new offer of employment. This provision applied if the player had refused to sign a new contract with his old club, and even if that club had no intention of playing him – or of paying him a salary – in the forthcoming season. Consequently, a club could in principle refuse to release a player's registration, and thereby prevent him from being able to play for another English League side. A player in such a position would be obliged to seek employment with a club in the (English) Southern League or (from 1890) the Scottish League, where the standard of play and the wages were lower but the clubs were not bound by the English league's punitive registration provisions. For most players, the alternative option was to quit the game altogether and return from whence they came – to full time employment in the mines, the factories, or the cotton industry.

This was the retain-and-transfer system, which treated players in the English League like little children; they should be seen and not heard, and if they complained too loudly about their lot then they'd be sent somewhere of sufficient depth or din, such as the coalmine or the factory floor, where their grumbling would be comfortably swallowed up. Combined with the fact that there was a cap on the maximum amount that players could earn, football clubs were in a position of complete control.

Until 1961, that is, when the maximum wage was swept away after vigorous and organised objection from the players' union, and, with the English League still groggy from this embarrassing defeat, there came the case of *Eastham v Newcastle*. George Eastham, then playing for Newcastle United, decided to challenge the status quo. On several occasions, Eastham had tried to leave his club for Arsenal after his contract had expired; though he was eventually allowed to make his move, his trade union asked him if he would take his dispute to court as a test case. The judge duly ruled that the retain-and-transfer system was illegal, calling it "so objectionable". Now, after a player's contract had expired, and his club still wanted him, he could move anywhere he liked so long as his club and the buying club agreed a fee.

The footballer would become truly emancipated in 1996. This was the year that the European Court of Justice ruled, in the case of *Belgian Football Association v Jean-Marc Bosman*, that if your contract had ended with a club and you wanted to leave, then you were free to go without the payment of a transfer fee – even if your club wanted to keep you. The European Court also ruled, for good measure, that it was illegal to restrict the amount of foreign players that could be included in any squad; for the previous five years, UEFA had insisted that the limit on such players was three.

New money

Pandora's six-yard box was now officially open. Once they were out of contract, players could move where they liked, and could earn as much money as they liked. Predictably, this wasn't to everyone's taste. For traditionalists, it drove a dagger through the heart of any notion of club loyalty. For some managers, meanwhile, it meant a loss of crucial control. As Brian Clough prophetically told his biographer Duncan Hamilton in *Provided You Don't Kiss Me*, "I'm telling you, in a few years' time, managers will have no power at all. We'll be redundant… The players will be in charge. They'll have wardrobes the size of houses, houses the size of castles and more cars than Formula One."

Other managers, however, didn't seem to mind too much. Bobby Campbell who, between 1976 and 1991 had managed Fulham, Portsmouth and Chelsea, was broadly supportive of this new world where leading players, often steered by rapacious agents, accrued millions of pounds during careers that lasted only a few seasons.

"They've become the rock stars, the film stars of today. And why not?... Players need help," he told me. "Players need help, because, basically, we all come from poor backgrounds. We're all poorly educated. We all have the gift of God to play football; so we play football because we love it, then people see we can play football, so we get offered a job as a professional... and then we're in a big, big world, and we're in with the sharks." The only caveat he offered, in partial agreement with Clough, was that "the one thing I wasn't happy with was the wage structure. I don't think there's half-a-dozen managers getting paid anywhere near what players are getting paid. [Notwithstanding that] players need help, they need assistance, to get what they deserve."

Whether or not the top players deserved it, they were certainly getting it; in fact, they were getting so much of it that you wondered whether many of them were struggling for motivation. They were receiving sums that were in danger of making them as apathetic as rock stars who'd just toured their second album; and a quick look at the list of the world's fifty highest paid footballers in 2008–09 revealed why.

This list, introduced by *Futebol Finance* in 2007–08, deserves a closer analysis. The first thing that was striking about the 2008–09 list was that it wasn't a list of the fifty best players in the world, but effectively a list of the fifty best football agents. Zlatan Ibrahimović who, the following season would move to Barcelona, had become known as "Ibracadabra" due to his wizardry with the ball; but his touch was nowhere as near magical as that of his agent, Mino Raiola, who had negotiated him a chart-topping weekly payout of £166,000 at Internazionale of Milan.

I'd seen these figures early one morning; and to see

Ibrahimović, albeit a multiple Serie A title winner, ahead of AC Milan's Kaka and Barcelona's Lionel Messi had been enough to shake off the last of my sleep. Apart from a handful of aberrations of that type – most notably, Tottenham's Darren Bent earning more than Roma's Francesco Totti – the names in both the '08 and '09 lists were in a fairly sensible pecking order: that is to say, they seemed reasonably reflective of the status of the players in the game, given either their past achievements or future prospects.

Specifically, it seemed fair enough that Paul Scholes was on a sum of £90,000 per week, just above Frank Ribéry's pay grade of £88,000 for the same period. Bayern Munich's Ribéry was on a rapid rise; Scholes was enjoying a blissful and nostalgic descent, occasionally footnoted by searing strikes – such as that decisive drive against Barcelona in the semi-final of the previous season's UEFA Champions League – that few others on earth could deliver.

On matters Barcelona, I was pleased to see that their midfielders, Xavi and Andrés Iniesta, were taking home the identical sum of £92,000 per week. My happiness wasn't only due to the fact that two often overlooked stars (at least until Spain's triumph in the Euro 2008 tournament) were being rewarded so thoroughly. It was also due to my confirmed suspicion that Xavi and Iniesta were in fact the same person; when they moved in towards goal, it was like an attack of the clones. Both were short and somewhat stocky, subtle in touch and timing of pass; they were the closest thing in football to frostbite in that their vision could fatally wound your defence long before it felt the slow thaw of realisation. The two often worked in such harmony that they seemed interchangeable, which is why £92,000 per week for each seemed cash relatively well spent.

Relatively, that is, in the head-shaking world of elite footballers' wages; but, as you're a manager, it's much of a much-ness to you. You're the tutor and mentor of athletes earning what Graeme Souness has, in typically succinct fashion, described as "F**k off money". "F**k off money" is an abstract concept, one which we can loosely define as the sort of sums that contrive to make an employee largely independent of his employer; or, in less polite terms, might entitle him to ask his manager, upon receipt of an unwelcome instruction, to "f**k off".

Yet it was difficult to know, in terms of earnings, precisely when the "F**k off" threshold had been reached. With reference to *Futebol Finance*'s list, it was clear that even the lowest earner, David Trezeguet of Juventus, was comfortably within the realm of obscene wealth, at £83,000 per week. What, then, was the lower limit? Was it £50,000 per week, or as low as £25,000? Perhaps the way to discern this boundary was as described by the American justice Potter Stewart, who wrote in the 1964 case of *Jacobellis v Ohio* that, whilst it was hard to define hard-core pornography, "I know it when I see it".

I looked at Sidney Govou's salary and I knew it when I saw it. Like Trezeguet, the Olympique Lyonnais right-winger was being paid £83,000 per week; or £332,000 per month, £3,984,000 per year. But unlike Trezeguet, Govou hadn't fulfilled the promise of his early career. During that phase, he had thrashed two astonishing efforts past Oliver Kahn in a UEFA Champions League victory, the Bayern Munich goalkeeper then the best in the world. One of those goals was a close-range swivel and shot that recalled Brazil's Romarío; the other, struck from twenty-five yards, was so swift that it was almost accompanied by a sonic boom.

Managing the rich

However, were we years later to have made an assessment of this promising student's career, the report card would read:

"Must do better". Our assessment would be initially glowing, but ultimately damning of Govou and his management. Superficially, he seemed to have flourished; a trophy-laden career, a one-club winger, reminiscent of what Ryan Giggs had done at Manchester United. He'd won seven consecutive *Ligue 1* championships, as well as a smattering of other cups here and there. He'd scored twice against the world champions Italy in a Euro 2008 qualifier. But, but, but.

During Lyon's period of unbroken dominance of the French league, between 2001 and 2008, they'd never advanced further than the UEFA Champions League quarter-finals; despite the promise of many more similarly explosive strikes, Govou had managed a strike-rate of only a goal every five games. £83,000 per week is the type of money you pay a player who is consistently making a difference at the very highest level; but when it came to Govou, it really didn't look like Lyon's president had got full bang for his buck.

So how did you get the best out of a Govou, from a player so much more naturally talented than most of those around him? If you're an ex-player, as are so many managers, then a short-term response would be to intimidate him with your own talent. Glenn Hoddle fell foul of this philosophy; when coaching England training sessions, he would assert his dominance over his players by first asking them to execute a series of difficult skills – which they could not – and then demonstrating them himself. While this served as a particularly effective form of humiliation, it wasn't the kind of thing that had his men charging out onto the Wembley turf, ready to die for the three lions on the shirt.

From player to manager

Perhaps for this reason there's a very long line of hugely successful footballers who go on to become hugely unsuccessful managers. Hoddle's achievements at Swindon and Chelsea were impressive, but they were some way short of the peaks that he reached as a player. (There's an ongoing debate about whether great players can make great managers; and, in the spirit of that debate, I'll keep it ongoing within these pages, by returning to it now and then in the chapters to come.) For now, though, there are a few things that strike me about this argument, and about why we're even having it.

The first thing is that we're greedy. Great players, by definition, have entertained us for several years on end, and have done so more successfully than most or all other forms of art that we've ever experienced. They've already delivered us moments that we scarcely dared to dream of. So our expectation that they should then go on and create sides as glorious as those they once graced is, well, asking a bit much. It's a little like listening over and over again to, say, Radiohead, and then mocking them because they never started a world-class record label, nurturing a stable of artists to their creative peak. Why, because their seminal albums *OK Computer*, *Kid A* and *In Rainbows* weren't thrilling enough to satisfy us?

If greed is perhaps a little strong – if we're only hoping, anxious and nostalgic, that they'll make great managers because of the joy they brought us on the pitch – then we should also prepare ourselves for disappointment. Because, as with the Radiohead example, they're almost entirely different jobs. Football management is of infinitely greater complexity than playing the game: coaching, coaxing a squad of twenty-odd players to immortality is tougher than the mere task of scoring a volley in the final of the UEFA Champions League. That's not to say that scoring is easy, no matter how simple Zinedine Zidane or Eusébio ever made it look; it's just that, compared to management, the passage to magnificence is much easier to map out.

However, whilst playing and managing are different jobs,

there are those who believe that, at the very highest level, you must have done the former if you're going to be any good at the latter. None have asserted this with more authority than Rinus Michels. In *Teambuilding*, Michels wrote that "at the world class level an additional quality is required. The Germans call it *fingerspitzengefühl*. It means intuitively knowing where the (football) shoe pinches. This cannot be learned at any coaching course. To be capable of reaching the absolute world class level, a coach must have gone through an extended experience as a top-level player."

Michels' point wasn't that you had to be a great player to be a great manager; he himself was a player of some, but not the utmost distinction, scoring 121 goals in 269 games for Ajax Amsterdam and playing five times for Holland. Moreover, there are only six people who have won the UEFA Champions League as a player and as a coach – Giovanni Trappatoni (AC Milan and Juventus), Miguel Muñoz (both with Real Madrid), Johan Cruyff (Ajax Amsterdam and FC Barcelona), Frank Rijkaard (Ajax Amsterdam and FC Barcelona), Pep Guardiola (both with FC Barcelona) and Carlo Ancelotti (both with AC Milan).

Michels was instead making the point that the highest levels of football are a particularly rarefied atmosphere, and you must have grown up knowing its nuances in order to flourish as a coach. Conversely, there's the opinion of Arrigo Sacchi: "I never realised that in order to become a jockey you have to have been a horse first... There's no rule. The most important thing is having the desire to keep improving." Yet, as we've seen in the chapter on Presence, there's no doubt that a successful career in the game stands you in excellent initial stead as a manager.

But back to the curious case of Sidney Govou. Another possible way to raise the game of gifted players like the Frenchman was to put them out of their comfort zones, and see whether they rose to the challenge. The career of Chelsea mainstay Frank Lampard was a classic case in point. During the seasons of 2001–02 and 2002–03, he scored eight and ten goals respectively; in the following two seasons, he scored nineteen and then twenty. His sudden spike in form coincided with the influx of owner Roman Abramovich's considerable millions, and a quality of player that had not consistently been seen at Stamford Bridge. More remarkably, Lampard saw them all off; in a club whose midfielders, during his career, have included Juan Sebastián Verón, Michael Ballack, Michael Essien, Claude Makélélé and more, he'd not only held his place, he'd thrived in it. Much of that was due to his own efforts, but the exponential improvement in his career coincided with the arrival at Chelsea of José Mourinho.

Mourinho put Lampard on a footballing pedestal, building the team around his diverse talents, and it's therefore unsurprising that Lampard has commented that "I think modern-day management is less about tactics and more about man-management. Look at the England job. England have got good players who win the Champions League and perform for their clubs week in, week out. The need is to make them feel that same confidence at international level. With England, our lack of confidence was obvious for everybody to see and I was part of that. That night against Croatia at Wembley, when we got knocked out [in the qualifying stages of Euro 2008], they started to move the ball about and we couldn't. We all felt that we were going to give the ball away every time we got it. That is how demoralised we had become with England."

I'd had two reactions to Lampard's words. The initial, visceral one was that it was strange to think of a footballer paid £150,000 per week or thereabouts needing anyone's approval. The second was that, *hang on a moment*, those players who *looked* scared out on that field *were* actually scared; there were times, watching England, when the players' body language was as if they'd just greeted the Grim Reaper on their front doorsteps.

That Croatia match, which England had to draw in order to go through to the finals of the tournament, was one that they lost 3–2, signalling the end of Steve McClaren's time in charge. In that contest, there was one passage of play that summed up the gulf in confidence between the two sets of players, and, by implication, the gulf in motivational skills between McLaren and his opposite number, Slaven Bilić. Fourteen minutes in, Croatia are already leading 1–0, beneficiaries of a horrendous piece of goal-keeping by Scott Carson. Eduardo da Silva flits across the top of the penalty area and rolls a short through-pass into the path of Ivica Olić, who rounds Carson to score Croatia's second; yet Olić is so confident that, at the moment he strikes the ball, he's looking away from the goal, and actually has to look again to check that the ball's entered the net.

How do you instil that level of self-belief in your players? I'd asked Gianluca Vialli, who'd been surprisingly frank in his response. "Well, I haven't been the best manager ever at doing that," he admitted, "because when I was player-manager I had very little experience and I thought that I was in a situation where I needed the players' help, rather than the other way round. Because I was young, and I was inexperienced, and I was under pressure, and they were my friends, so I was expecting them to help me, rather than the other way round. Obviously I was trying to lead by example, and I was trying to motivate them all the time, but they were expecting me to be already good enough to deal with all the pressure."

Vialli's experience was an unusual one in that he'd taken over as Chelsea manager during his playing career. "It was extremely tough for me," he said. "Because I had to manage myself, and train myself, I had to be right up here (he tapped his head), but also I had to keep an eye on all the players in training and make sure that they were motivated. So I had one salary, but I was actually doing two jobs. Because I needed to be ready as a player, to look after myself, but I also needed to look after the players. So I managed to do that for a year and a half, and then I was still player-manager, but by my last season I very, very, very rarely picked myself."

How The Anfield Rap ruined Liverpool

Of all the people to whom I spoke, of all the sources that I saw, read and listened to, Vialli was the second most helpful in showing me the highs and lows of being a player-manager. The most helpful, without question, was the appearance of Kenny Dalglish in "The Anfield Rap". For those of you who've not yet experienced it, "The Anfield Rap" was the song that Liverpool FC, then the perennial league champions, released just prior to the 1988 FA Cup final against Wimbledon. I hadn't watched it for several years, was slightly fearful of doing so, and so it was with some trepidation that I brought it up on YouTube.

There were no words for the terror that it brought to the ears. I'd always been someone who sensed acutely the embarrassment of others, which is why comedies of humiliation such as *Some Mothers Do 'Ave 'Em* and *The Office* had never sat well with me. When I watched others suffer onscreen, I would always find myself deeply experiencing their pain. So it was that after eleven seconds of the track, my eyes were streaming with tears, a spontaneous response to the screen and the horror that unfolded there.

By that time, a tinny and minimal rap beat had long since dropped, and was burrowing its way into my soul. By that time, John Barnes had begun throwing jerky head-nods and strange hand signals as if his stereotype allowance depended on it. Then, miraculously – following a silent cameo from goalkeeper Bruce Grobbelaar, who was later to reappear to devastating effect – there were five seconds of beauty, in the form of some supreme spoken word from Bill Shankly. "My idea," came that stirring growl, "was to build Liverpool into a bastion of invincibility."

Then the hook kicked in – "You'll-Never-Walk-Alone" – which was respectable enough, which actually seemed to flow with the beat for a time, and it seemed that we were out of the woods. But then, at thirty-six seconds, one of Liverpool's players, clad, as were the rest of them, in a shellsuit touched by brash fluorescence and a cap at forty-five degrees to the horizon, threw some robotics, and the game was up. The remaining three minutes passed in a flurry of popping, locking, Ray-Bans and medallions, interrupted only and mercifully by a reel of spectacular football highlights, which were in fact so good that they almost redeemed all that had gone before.

There's no greater evidence that black players suffer discrimination in football than in the disproportionate attention paid to the verse of John Barnes on this track. Lyrically, Bruce Grobbelaar, John Aldridge and Steve McMahon do themselves no favours here, but it's Barnes who gets truly flayed by critics for his part in this enterprise; even though it lasts only fifteen seconds or so, and is largely factually accurate: "I come from Jamaica, my name is John Barn-es/When I do my thing the crowd go bananas". Prior to this, however, he had produced the lines "You two Scousers are always yapping/I'm gonna show you some serious rapping", after which his credibility was very much hanging in the balance. I suppose that, with hip-hop being part of the black heritage, people just expected Barnes to come with a stronger game than that.

"The Anfield Rap" reached number three in the charts. But I don't think, at the time, that people bought it wholly out of a sense of irony; I think they actually liked it. Much as I could mock the lyrics, I had to applaud Kenny Dalglish for the team spirit that he'd built. There Dalglish was, standing (in fairness, somewhat bashfully) as part of the crowd as they freestyled their way into legend; he was in charge of one of the most successful sides in history, and one of the reasons for their sustained brilliance must be that they were close-knit enough to make a tune like "The Anfield Rap".

But there was a flipside to this friendliness, and it was pointed out by Bob Paisley, by then a club director. "There's no room for sentiment [as a manager]," he said. "I was a big softie until it came to what was good for the club. Then I could be as hard as nails. And Kenny can't afford to let his heart rule his head. It's OK being the nice guy but he's got to get rid of some players before they start to believe they have still got a future at Liverpool."

Paisley, as we saw in the chapter on Vision, called Liverpool's decline long before anyone else did; and it's possible that "The Anfield Rap" was to blame. An essential part of the manager's job is to break up a winning team, to ensure effective transition to a line-up of fresher minds and legs whilst maintaining dominance over rivals. That's something which it's much harder to achieve if, at the same time that you should be thinking about selling your players, you're laughing, joking and break-dancing with them.

Dalglish's powers of motivation were there for all to see, both in the video and in the results – two league titles and an FA Cup – that he achieved in three seasons. He would also go on to manage Blackburn Rovers to a league championship in 1995. But was he missing a ruthlessness that would have made him even better? *The Harvard Business Review on Motivating People* (Harvard Business School Press, 2003) states that:

Managers fall into three motivational groups. Those in the first, affiliative managers, need to be liked more than they need to get things done. Their decisions are aimed at increasing their own popularity rather than promoting the goals of the organization. Managers motivated by the need to achieve – the second group – aren't worried about what people think of them. They focus on setting goals and reaching them, but they put their own achievement and recognition first. Those in the third group – institutional managers – are interested above all in power. Recognizing that you get things done in organizations only if you can influence the people around you, they focus on building power through influence rather than through their own individual achievement. People in this third group are the most effective, and their direct reports have a greater sense of responsibility, see organizational goals more clearly, and exhibit more team spirit.

In summary: nice guys finish last. The downfall of player-managers was due to the fact that, as far as Harvard Business School's categories went, they fell into the affiliative category; having grown too close to their co-workers, they were ultimately more keen to please than to prosper. As a manager, it's best to maintain a degree of distance from your followers; footballers are constantly trying to get the measure of you, and so to some extent you must remain inscrutable, whilst being highly agile in your thinking. Rinus Michels noted as much in *Teambuilding*:

With the psychological team building process every coach must realize this statement is true: "what works today, is not guaranteed to work tomorrow". In this domain, there are no guarantees. Therefore the coach must continually remain alert. Every day there can be internal or external factors that can influence the team mentality of the players. This causes a constant change of the tension level.

Racehorses, hedgehogs, children and chickens

In *Sven-Göran Eriksson on Football*, a book that the then England manager co-wrote with psychologist and fellow Swede Willi Railo, the authors considered that the majority of leading professional footballers were far more insecure than they were letting on. They identified that footballers fell into

> four personality types [A, B, C and D], with different strengths of ambition and performance anxiety… A has great ambition and high performance anxiety. B has great ambition, but is not afraid of failing. C has little ambition and is afraid of making mistakes. D has little ambition, but is also not bothered about failing… A is the type who is fine in ordinary league matches but fades away when it really matters. B is, not surprisingly, the type who makes the most of his resources. B dares to excel when it really matters. So, it's a question of working to be a B type and creating a B culture, and this we do by stimulating ambition and reducing fear.

Eriksson and Railo contended that the most common personality type by far – some 80 per cent – was type A, which explained England's capitulation in that qualifier against Croatia, and Lampard's admission that, in front of an expectant Wembley crowd, they'd been afraid to receive the ball. If we take that figure of 80 per cent as broadly accurate, then a manager is in an unusual position; he has to earn sufficient confidence from them so that they'll trust him with their egos, but at the same time he can't be their friend.

How, then, should he relate to them? Reasonably enough, some managers have treated their players as humans. "Beyond the footballer there is a person who likes to be considered, he likes to be treated properly, and if you can get this kind of relationship in the right way then they will give everything for you," Zola told me (somewhat refreshingly, I must add).

"[It's] the kind of respect that goes beyond football, it's just a matter of life. If you treat people well, they will respond to what you're asking from them."

Other managers have regarded their players as animals of the field or the farm. Guy Roux, speaking to *L'Équipe* in 1996 after his Auxerre team had won a domestic double of the Ligue 1 championship and the Coupe de France, told the publication that "this is the first year that the players have believed in me. When I decide something, they are more receptive… Before, I had a few hedgehogs and chickens. Now, the hedgehogs have all left. And chickens are animals endowed with intelligence. When I was small and went into the yard they used to run away. But, as soon as my granddad arrived, they charged towards him, because he was the one who gave them their feed. Certain of my players in the past didn't understand that it was me who was giving out the feed."

It wasn't particularly flattering to be either a hedgehog or a chicken; the former was, if cute, rather slow-witted, whilst the latter was certainly less cute, and arguably not witted at all. Players of more fragile psyches would have preferred Bob Paisley's analogy, which was far more flattering; he'd compared elite footballers to thoroughbred racehorses, highly gifted yet highly sensitive to changes in their immediate atmosphere. However, this empathy didn't make Paisley any more inclined than Roux to wrap them in cotton wool; it just meant that he was probably even better at knowing which buttons to push. For example, as related in *Passing Rhythms: Liverpool FC and the Transformation of Football* (ed. John Williams, Stephen Hopkins and Cathy Long), Paisley once arranged for one of his players, Tommy Smith, a hard man of formidable reputation to be given "the wrong pre-match meal… so that he was in a suitably bad mood for the match."

If typecasting your players as hedgehogs, chickens or racehorses isn't your thing, then you can always treat them like children; and, since plenty of players over the years have referred to managers as father figures, this might be a philosophy worth adopting. Of course, there are many ways to play this role. Wayne Rooney referred to Fabio Capello as a "strict father", whilst one of Capello's fellow Italians was more likely to be seen as the doting sort. During my preparatory reading for an interview with Gianfranco Zola, I was struck that the only thing that matched his pride in his players was his faith in them. He had, it seemed, a genuine affection for them, which made him closest in style among then Premier League managers to Arsenal's Wenger. His players, for their part, spoke effusively about the confidence he had given them in their ability, a form of nurturing that came naturally to Zola; certainly, he regarded this as the most rewarding part of his job. "I think that is the best feeling," he said, "when you work with a young player, with [James] Tomkins, or [Jack] Collison, or with Carlton Cole; you spend time and energy, you really want them desperately to succeed; and then you see them doing very well."

Much of Zola's closeness with his players seemed to come from his humility; much has been remarked about his unassuming demeanour, and the most revealing part of my conversation with him wasn't in what he said, but what he did. Following a Friday afternoon press conference, he, the club's press officer and I had gone into his office for the aforementioned interview. The room was a strange shape and size; it was cavernous with a low ceiling, and looked more like the waiting room to an office than an office itself, with a desk in the corner and two sofas with their backs to opposite walls. Greg, the press officer, sat down behind Zola's desk, while Zola and I took a sofa each. The problem was that we were a good eight feet apart; and so, to put this right, Zola pulled a seat over in front of me and perched there, nodding attentively as I asked each question. He reminded me of me in a lecture theatre several years previously, waiting anxiously on the next words of my favourite law professor.

Odd as it might seem, I didn't see this as remarkable until a few hours later. By then, I had tried to imagine any of the other Premier League managers sitting on a raised chair before me, smiling patiently at my questions. And I couldn't; and that's what made Zola different, and maybe special. You could just as easily see him kicking about with kids in the local park as you could see him trading kick-ups with Maradona, and it was for this simple and lasting reason that he was adored. For him, there was no particular secret to his methods: "You just talk to them, reassure them, motivate them… sometimes, tell them off; it's an everyday job, you need to be there all the time, you can't afford to let it slip out of your hands. It's consistent motivation."

When it came to making his players perform, Zola preferred the path of pleasant incentives; after all, that's what had worked best in his playing career. "I think one of the biggest things I wanted when I was a footballer was when a manager would come to me and he gave me responsibilities; when he said, 'Okay, Gianfranco, today you need to produce something special.' I felt great about that. I think it was a very great thing, [better] than telling me, 'Okay, Gianfranco, do this, this, this, this'…" said Zola, his gaze surged this way and that as he saw some imaginary manager's chalk flitting across a blackboard.

Dr Maslin, Fabio Capello, and boot camp

Empowerment was all very well, but, as a parent, there are many other ways to ensure your children's compliance with orders. In 2004 Dr Bonnie Maslin, a New York-based psychologist, wrote *Picking Your Battles: Winning Strategies for Raising Well-Behaved Kids*: in one of her chapters, she set out two attitudes to parenthood that could just as easily be applied to man management:

"Welcome to Boot Camp" parents advocate an iron-fisted philosophy, convinced that the family container only needs to be strong and muscular, but not very elastic. Holding an icy, tight, hard-nosed grip over children, they misguidedly regard love and affection as unnecessary coddling… Expecting children to listen and obey unquestioningly, they fail to listen to their children or encourage autonomy.

In Dr Maslin's next paragraph, she set out a parental ethos that seemed to have much in common with Fabio Capello's approach to the England job:

It's all in the delivery: if you use your anger to teach, so that your child sees cause and effect in their misbehavior, that is a consequence-and-cost response. If your anger is used to vent and "make your child pay" for misconduct with suffering, that's punishment. Punishment never works to change or improve behavior. Consequences and cost offer guidance – the only effective route to discipline. The next time his behavior goes awry, start saying to your child, "There will be consequences for your actions," not threatening, "You will be punished for what you have done."

The Capello way was, generally speaking, that there should not be punishment for the sake of punishment; whilst not soft with his players, there was a clear rationale behind any harsh and corrective measures – substitution, or dropping altogether – that he would take against them. On the other hand, the "Welcome to Boot Camp" approach as described by Dr Maslin was once all too common in British football: an unsubtle, one-size-fits-all stance that involved a great deal of ranting and aimless tests of manhood.

The reason Boot Camp died as a method was that it

was ineffective: it generally didn't bring positive responses from players, who succeeded in spite of it. One who wasn't so fortunate was a professional who'd played for Sheffield Wednesday under Trevor Francis between 1991 and 1995. Francis had enjoyed a successful start to his career at the Hillsborough club, finishing third in the top flight in his first season, and then reaching the finals of the FA Cup and the League Cup in the following year, both of which Wednesday would lose to Arsenal. He would be dismissed in his final season, having finished fifteenth in the top division. Given his club's resources, this seemed a reasonable enough return. However, according to one of his former players, who asked not to be named, Francis' man management skills had been sorely lacking in several areas, with the result that, one day, he'd done what no manager could afford to do; he'd "lost the dressing-room".

By contrast, he'd had nothing but praise for one of Trevor Francis' assistants. "One of the best people [at Sheffield Wednesday] was Frank Barlow. He was the reserve team coach but he helped out with the first team. He was brilliant... He was old-school. He used to play for Sheffield United back in the 1960s and 1970s, and he was one of those 'bruiser' players who'd kick you into Row G as soon as he got the chance. And the players knew that. And I think you need that underbelly of fear all the time as a manager. [As a player] you need to know that he doesn't have one doubt in his mind that he could axe you from the team, he could criticise you, and no one would do anything about it. The minute that you give players that idea that they're in the side all the time, that they're always going to be first-choice, they can do what they want, then that's when you lose the dressing-room."

The devil's advocate might argue here that this player, given the career path that he'd gone on to take, was never really cut out for the emotional demands of football at the highest level. That's arguable; however, he'd also shown sufficient fortitude to have represented his country at youth level, and so the evidence pointed the finger at Francis' poor handling of matters. A greater degree of understanding could have been expected from him; after all, Francis had been a promising young talent himself, having first appeared for Birmingham City aged sixteen, and scoring four goals in a First Division match before his seventeenth birthday.

In further mitigation, it was also possible that Francis had overstayed his welcome at Sheffield Wednesday; five years, after all, is a long time for any manager to spend in the same post. Bela Guttmann, who'd coached Benfica to successive European Cup triumphs in 1961 and 1962, had believed that it was "fatal" for a manager to spend more than two seasons at any club; whilst Paul Simpson, the editor of *Champions* magazine, had told me that "I think there is a time limit for coaches with players. I remember talking to Alan Smith when he started writing for *FourFourTwo*, and he said that the problem with George Graham towards the end of his time at Arsenal was that you could predict what he was going to come out with. You were sitting there and you weren't intimidated, you were just bored."

When all's said and done, though, it's still surprising that Francis, who in 1979 had been the first player in England to cost £1million when Brian Clough signed him from Birmingham, and would go on to win two European Cups at the City Ground, had apparently failed to adopt the nuanced outlook to man management that had been Clough's hallmark.

Clough and Revie

Then again, perhaps that would have been asking too much: the Nottingham Forest manager had a peerless intuition where players were concerned. As Clough told Duncan Hamilton in

Provided You Don't Kiss Me, "I can tell, from the moment I see someone in the dressing room, whether he's off colour, had a row with his missus, kicked the cat or just doesn't fancy it that particular day. I know who needs lifting. I know who needs to have his arse kicked. I know who needs leaving alone to get on with it. It only takes a minute to score a goal, and it takes less than a minute to change someone's outlook with a word or two. That's just another form of coaching that you won't find in the manuals, which is why I've never read them. It's a special kind of coaching done only by very, very good managers – like me."

Clough continued: "You have to know what the people working with you are thinking, and you have to sense their mood. You have to read minds, and second-guess them. You have to see right into a player. And then the trick – if it is a trick – is to say exactly the right thing at exactly the right time. Or you just shut up and sit in silence."

Gianluca Vialli had worked with several managers whose personal touch, like Clough's, was second to none. They'd included Vujadin Boskov, the underrated Serb who'd taken Sampdoria to a Serie A title in 1991, and to the European Cup final in 1992, losing by a single goal to Barcelona; and Marcello Lippi, whom Vialli described simply as "my Messiah". Yet his most telling anecdote concerning the bespoke approach that a manager should take to each player came from a man who was often compared to Clough.

"You've got to have rules for everybody," Vialli told me, "but you can't treat everybody the same way. For example, I was speaking to [José] Mourinho about that; [he said] if you've got a player like John Terry, you can tell him 'You were shit on Sunday', and you'll expect him to react in such a way that he's going to be the best player on the pitch in the following game. If you have another player, and I think he mentioned someone like [William] Gallas, and you say,

'Look, you were shit on Sunday', then you're going to lose him for about a month, because he's not good enough to take that, his personality is not [right]."

Being all things to all men in this fashion is something that requires a great deal of concentration; it also calls for great acting skills. The lasting critique of the manager who merely stands there and rails at his players is that he has only one gear, one tempo. He becomes a parody of himself, like any of those Hollywood action heroes who don't realise that they're no longer terrifying, and carry on making edgy thrillers in their sixties whilst their more realistic contemporaries have found more rewarding careers in ironic comedy, playing with their grandchildren, or sunbathing. To be a manager of the first rank, you must be able to adapt; from father figure to benevolent dictator to confidante, to confidence trickster, to comedian; all roles essential to your efforts at creating team spirit.

There seemed to have been no one better at doing so than Don Revie. The more that I saw or read of him, whether in works of fiction such as David Peace's *The Damned United*, in biographies or documentaries, the more I was impressed by the loyalty his players showed to him, long after his death. Their regard for him, as a group, at least equalled that shown by former Liverpool players towards Shankly and Paisley; when he was criticised publicly, they were tigerish in defence of his legacy. I went, then, to speak with John Faulkner, who'd been at Leeds United during their period of dominance in the 1960s and 1970s.

Faulkner had first come across Revie in 1970, when Leeds had been drawn in the FA Cup against non-league Sutton United, for whom Faulkner played centre-back. Leeds won the tie 6–0; but Revie, impressed by how well Faulkner had acquitted himself against his attack, signed him shortly afterwards as a ready replacement for Jack Charlton. Faulkner, who was now an independent business consultant and a visiting fellow at the Cranfield University School of Management, told me the story of his move to Leeds, which shed some valuable light on Revie's dedication to his players, and threw up an ode to the etiquette of Bill Nicholson.

Nicholson, the Scot who in the 1960–61 season led Tottenham Hotspur to the first "Double" since 1897 – a triumph in the First Division and the FA Cup in the same year – was a man renowned for his excellent manners. Faulkner, at that time faced with a flurry of offers from Leeds, Arsenal, Crystal Palace and Tottenham, remained grateful years later for Nicholson's decorum.

"It was getting so confusing," said Faulkner. "I thought it was going to be either Arsenal, because I'd supported them as a kid, or Leeds, because they were the ones who came in for me; and I was going to have to tell Crystal Palace and Tottenham." So he called Tottenham, and left a message thanking Nicholson for his interest, but that he had decided to go to Arsenal. "He wrote me the most beautiful letter," said Faulkner, "and it went something like this: 'John; well done to you, that's a very mature decision you've made. Really hope you do well in the future, and thank you very much for not getting us involved when you wouldn't have come here in the first place.' It showed what kind of a manager he was, that he would take the time [to do that]."

Faulkner then went to meet Bertie Mee, who was in charge at Arsenal, and it finally looked as though the North London club would obtain Faulkner's signature; but Leeds United's manager had other ideas. "Revie was very clever," said Faulkner, his voice briefly slipping into a conspiratorial whisper, as if in homage to the manner of Revie's approach. Revie had tracked down his telephone number, called him personally, and arranged to meet him in clandestine, although slightly comic, circumstances: "In the Wimpey bar opposite the Royal Gardens Hotel in Kensington," said Faulkner. "He was quite a secretive sort of guy... but I think I'd much rather have been in the Kensington Royal Gardens!"

Pausing the moment there, I could see the scene: Faulkner, the looming centre-back, on the verge of football fame, looking wistfully across the road at that hotel, the symbol of the glory and high life to come; and a crouching Revie, muttering, hiding his cloak-and-dagger offer to join Leeds beneath the helpful crackle of greaseproof paper.

In truth, of course, Revie was more relaxed than that, and was probably just cutting costs; what's more, being offered fast food on your first date is just about alright, if you know that champagne and caviar are somewhere soon down the line. Given that Leeds had an upcoming FA Cup semi-final against Manchester United, Revie thought Faulkner might like to go and watch the game, and offered him and his girlfriend tickets. The match was to take place at Hillsborough, Sheffield Wednesday's ground, and Revie asked if Faulkner could meet him there an hour before the match, so that he could give him the tickets in person. Rising early, Faulkner and his other half travelled up to South Yorkshire, reached the stadium, and waited in the car park for the arrival of the Leeds United coach.

"The coach turns up; and of course it's the semi-final of the FA Cup, it's packed, everywhere's packed. 'Get yourself near the coach, because it'll be crowded,' [Revie had] said, 'and I'll get off, and give you the tickets.'" As Faulkner related the next part of the story, he still sounded faintly amazed by what then happened. "Every single one of the players, as they got off, came over and said, 'Hey John! Nice to see you, well done for being up here! Hope you enjoy the game!' I mean, this is Billy Bremner, this is Jack Charlton, this is Norman Hunter – Norman Hunter was my hero – and then Revie came across, gave me the two tickets, we wished each other the best, and then off he went."

This made a pivotal impression on Faulkner, and having signed for Leeds, he asked his now colleagues, Bremner, Charlton and Hunter among them, about their recollections of this career-changing event. "I said to the players, 'You know that semi-final day?'" smiled Faulkner. "'Aah, yeah,' they said, 'Revie said, "When you get off, make a point of saying hello to John out there. We're trying to sign him".'"

The team bonding would continue over the next two years; although Faulkner would play only four times for the first team before being transferred to Luton Town, he and other regular reserve team players were all made to feel central to Revie's thinking. In a small but significant move, for example, Revie ensured that the first team and reserve team shared dressing-rooms before training, instead of allowing them to change separately.

"[Revie's] thing was family. And he didn't just say it, he enacted it," said Faulkner, who wasn't uncritical of this. "He'd sorted out the whole city of Leeds around football. If there were any players who'd got up to anything, they phoned him, and he dealt with it. So he talked to the police about it; [he'd say] 'Get me out of bed, no matter what time.' And he did it. There were a few scrapes – there were a few lively players at Leeds, big characters – and he would get out of bed, five o'clock, four o'clock in the morning, and go out and sort it out."

There's the faintest hint of the Mafia about someone who'll protect their men at any cost, who has the police, if not at his beck and call, then turning a blind eye to his activities. Revie's sense of solidarity was extreme, almost military in its resolve; it was reminiscent of the ethos of the US Rangers, that no man should be left behind on the battlefield. Regardless of how much football has evolved over the years, a manager's fidelity to his players is the core of his authority. There are times when that fidelity will make a manager almost criminally culpable or seem merely childish, as on the umpteen occasions when he claims not to have witnessed a clear infringement of the rules by one of his men.

Stand by your men

That's the starkest choice a manager must make between public and private approval. If he offers a confessional on television in front of millions of watching viewers, admitting that yes, he saw and was appalled by that two-footed and London-bus-late challenge by his centre-back that put their centre forward out for a season, then he earns the respect of the public for his honesty. But then he must return to the icily silent dressing-room, to a group of eleven people who have put their hopes in his hands for ninety minutes, knowing that he can't honestly look them in the eyes and tell them that he would take their side against the world watching, judging, out there.

Honesty – or, in this context, betrayal – was Glenn Hoddle's cardinal sin as England manager. Hoddle was dismissed in February 1999 for comments widely construed to mean that disabled people were merely suffering the effects of bad karma from a previous life. The ensuing furore, including a recommendation from the then Prime Minister, did for Hoddle in the eyes of the public; but, in truth, it seemed that he had lost the faith of several of his players long before. The previous summer Hoddle had seen his team eliminated from the second round of the 1998 World Cup in France, on penalties, by Argentina; he'd also seen, in the eighteen-year-old Michael Owen, the emergence of a major world star. What few people in the public domain anticipated was Hoddle's publication of a fully frank and therefore wholly insensitive diary of the tournament's events, co-written, inexplicably, by David Davies, the Public Affairs Director of the FA.

Hoddle seemed to have been trying to set some kind of world record for arson: on almost every page, there was a burnt bridge. On page 52, he told the world that Darren Anderton had seen a faith healer for help with mental health issues; on page 53, we were treated to the news that Paul Merson had family problems. On page 69, Andy Cole's England career under Hoddle died an undignified death, with Hoddle declaring that "he still needs three or four opportunities in front of goal before he takes one, and you don't get that many at international level".

David Beckham, we learned, had a "vagueness" about him, probably caused by his preoccupation with his girlfriend Victoria, and throughout the book we witnessed the gradual disintegration of Paul Gascoigne's psyche – despite Hoddle giving him "love and discipline" – which resulted in Gascoigne's omission from the final World Cup squad. *Glenn Hoddle: My World Cup Diary* wasn't just a field day for the tabloids, it was a festival: instead of having to dig through dustbins or sniff out tip-offs for that week's headlines, all they had to do was copy and paste. Never had the media mountain come so spectacularly to Mohammed.

You wouldn't have caught Don Revie doing such a diary; or Sir Alex Ferguson, for that matter. Faulkner, as part of his business consultancy, worked at the University of Warwick, in sessions for their Certificate in Applied Management course; in preparation for these, he had interviewed Ferguson about his principles of management. Having spent a day with him, he was in no doubt as to the key to Ferguson's success. "His big thing is loyalty. There's a beautiful story that I was part of," Faulkner said, and proceeded to tell me the following tale, which didn't say everything there was to say about a man as complex as the Scot, but which certainly said enough.

Bryan Gunn was the goalkeeper when I was at Norwich [as assistant manager], and he was an apprentice at Aberdeen when Ferguson was their manager. Ferguson had three sons, and he used to get the apprentices to babysit them when he and his wife went out; so Bryan Gunn used to babysit them, and earn a couple of quid.

Bryan Gunn didn't really make it at Aberdeen, so he went off to Norwich where he really made a great career, and played for Scotland; Ferguson went off to Manchester United. Gunn got married, and had two kids – a little boy, and a little girl – and the little boy got leukaemia, and died. So the whole club went to the funeral; we're all in the church, and Ferguson turns up. He gets in at the back of the church, waits for the funeral to finish, goes up to Gunn and his wife, gives them his condolences, and then he was off. He wouldn't speak to any reporters, wouldn't speak to anybody else; he was back in his car, and off to Manchester United.

So I said to Bryan afterwards; "Did you know he was coming?" "No," said Bryan, "I knew that he knew that my son had leukaemia, but he hadn't mentioned anything to me." He made the effort to go from one side of the country to the other side of the country because he needed to be there. Not a phone call, not a telegram; just that extra mile you go, and I think that makes him the manager that he is. He goes the extra mile.

LUCK

Jock Stein was the Dick Whittington of Scottish football. If you were to call Stein simply the greatest manager that Britain ever had, you might be underselling him. Stein, who made his name as a Protestant in charge of Glasgow Celtic, a passionately Catholic club, won no less than twenty-six major trophies between 1960 and 1985, including, in 1967, the first ever European Cup by a team from the United Kingdom. In his glorious career, just over half of which he spent at Celtic, he more than anyone made Scottish football a respected force, and often a feared one.

But Jock Stein was also Dick Whittington, in that his fairytale, but for one timely intervention, may never have come to pass. According to legend, Dick Whittington, a young man who'd been raised in poverty, went to London to find his fortune; having heard that the streets there were paved with gold, he was crestfallen to find that they were instead riven with rejection and despair. Whittington, having received an apparently mortal blow to his confidence, packed his meagre belongings and prepared to return to obscurity – only, on his way out of town, to hear the famous Bow Bells ring out, summoning him back with the vow that he would be three times voted mayor of London. Whittington returned; and a future that he'd scarcely dared to hope for was his.

Unlike Whittington, Stein hadn't sought out the promise

offered by the big city, but had moved many hundred miles to a small town to find a better life. Raised in the working-class town of Burnbank, Stein began work as a miner but his footballing ability soon led him further afield to play the game full-time in 1950 for the Welsh non-league team Llanelli. Whilst his side was much the better for his presence, his wife became increasingly homesick, and Stein himself faced the frustration of being refused a move to one of the leading teams in England, rumoured to be Wolverhampton Wanderers.

The young Scotsman, as his biographer Archie Macpherson tells us, resigned himself to failure: Macpherson asks us, at that crucial point in his life, to "picture a dejected Stein mentally packing his bags, feeling like the bankrupt whose investment has turned sour, bracing himself for heading back to a lifestyle he thought he had left for ever". But then Jock Stein had his Dick Whittington moment. Jimmy Gribben, a scout at Glasgow Celtic, had been asked to find a defender as a backup for their first team. Having watched Stein at his previous club, Albion Rovers, in a 3–0 loss to Celtic, he asked for Stein's whereabouts; having tracked him down in Wales, he made him an offer.

The signing was greeted with derision by Celtic fans, with dismay by Stein's Protestant friends – many of whom stopped speaking to him – but Stein himself would never forget its significance. He went on to captain Celtic and, of course, to manage them; he showed his gratitude to Gribben by visiting him in the club's boot-room with the European Cup as soon as he had returned with it from Lisbon. Stein knew that but for Gribben, whose call for him rang out as clearly as the Bow Bells, he could have spent his next few decades down the mines, grafting away his daylight hours in darkness.

However, we can't push this sort of analysis too far; there are already too many fanciful "what if?" scenarios associated with the game of football. As David Goldblatt relates in *The*

Ball is Round, "Gustáv Sebes, coach of the Hungarian Golden Team [who lost the 1954 World Cup final 3–2 to Germany] claimed in retrospect that, 'If Hungary had won the football World Cup there would have been no counter revolution but a powerful thrust in the building of socialism in the country.'" Having said that, there's something about the nature of football – the fact that the slightest deflection, or the most marginal of offside decisions, can alter the course of an entire season – that makes its managers all too prone to wondering what might have been.

The strange fate of AFC Wimbledon

There are some people who believe that football is driven by mysterious and supernatural forces; that, around the terraces of each village ground or under the floodlights of every city stadium, the air hangs heavy with the rumblings of the occult. How else can one explain the perennial recurrence of penalty awards against one's team; that last-minute attempt at an equaliser, firmly on target for the top corner, which suddenly falters in its flight and then drifts wistfully wide of the far post? Such people offer themselves up to the forces in prayer, ritual or both, knowing that no matter how diligently they might prepare for a game, they're much better off if they make a friend of fate.

Helenio Herrera, the great coach of FC Barcelona and Internazionale of Milan, wasn't one of them. In *Inverting the Pyramid*, Jonathan Wilson wrote that the Argentine was "dismissive of the concept of luck in football. 'I hate it when they talk about being fortunate,' said Herrera towards the end of his all-conquering career. 'I don't believe in good luck. When someone has won so much in twenty years, can it be fortune? Modestly, I've won more than any other manager in the world. My case is unprecedented.'"

Herrera's view, if not modest, was unequivocal. What's more, had he come down to Watford FC's training ground to oversee our training session with Aidy Boothroyd, he would have been delighted by an edict he found on one of the message boards. THERE IS NO SUCH THING AS LUCK. THIS WRONGLY USED WORD IS SIMPLY A POSITIVE BY-PRODUCT OF HARD WORK. Herrera's own style had been to pin bold statements to the walls of his dressing room, and Watford had followed in that proud tradition.

Elsewhere on this message board, there could be found a steadily evangelical fervour. Beneath the heading THE GOD OF FOOTBALL, there were all sorts of directives, mostly consisting of don'ts; a set of secular commandments, followed by a slightly startling penal code. NON-NEGOTIABLES, barked the message board, were LATENESS... INTENSITY... TIDINESS. Then, adding a sanction that was as vague as it was threatening, it said PERSISTENT OFFENDERS WILL BE PUNISHED PHYSICALLY BY THEIR PEERS. Last, best and most literary was the ominous declaration that WHAT WE DO IN THE DARK WILL COME TO THE LIGHT. THE GOD OF FOOTBALL SEES EVERYTHING.

From the message board, it seemed that the God of Football, whoever and wherever he was, didn't have much time for luck either; that he sneered at the very thought of it. However, if he'd paid much attention to the end of AFC Wimbledon's 2008–09 season, then he wouldn't have been so sure of himself: their experience, during the final weeks of their championship campaign was a case study in the very best and worst of footballing fortune that a club could have.

Before that, though, we should take a quick look at AFC Wimbledon's brief history. They'd been founded as recently as 2002; the previous club that represented their town, Wimbledon FC, had been established in 1889, and had enjoyed remarkable success, rising from the non-leagues to their highest finish of sixth in the old First Division and even winning the FA Cup in 1988, with a famous 1–0 victory over Liverpool. However, Wimbledon FC's demise was imminent. The Taylor Report on stadium safety, commissioned in the wake of the 1989 Hillsborough disaster, recommended that each First Division club should play in an all-seater stadium, which necessitated Wimbledon FC's move from their old home, Plough Lane.

So far, so sensible. The problem came when Wimbledon FC, in a decision that was almost universally despised, chose to move to Milton Keynes, alienating their loyal fan base at a stroke. Whilst Wimbledon FC would stutter into administration, being rescued by a buyer who would rename it the MK Dons, the fans who it had left behind formed their own club, AFC Wimbledon, to be based in South London and remain forever true to its roots.

AFC Wimbledon had enjoyed a superb start to its life, with four promotions in seven years, including three championships. It had risen through two leagues, the Combined Counties and the Isthmian, and now as I went to visit them, stood at the top of the Blue Square Conference South, just two promotions away from the Football League itself. But, all of a sudden, getting there wasn't proving so easy.

I found out as much when I spoke with AFC Wimbledon's manager, Terry Brown. Brown, as it turned out, was experiencing – literally – a phenomenon known as "squeaky-bum time"; a phrase coined by Sir Alex Ferguson, and defined by the *Collins English Dictionary* as "the tense final stages of a league competition, especially from the point of view of the leaders". "The fact that I've won three titles before at this level, and taken clubs up before, doesn't make it any less [stressful]," winced Brown. "I've been in the toilet two times today, and normally I'm a once-a-day man!... You can kid yourself, but your body doesn't lie, does it?"

Brown's body was currently producing inconvenient truths because he and AFC Wimbledon had recently endured not one but two bouts of spectacular misfortune, both of which were "burning away" at him even as we spoke. "We've had certain injustices against us over the last month," he railed. "There was a refereeing decision at Weston-super-Mare where it cost us; and one at Eastleigh where a 6ft 6in guy literally punched the ball, and the referee who's right behind him gives the goal, and they beat us."

It wasn't that I didn't believe Brown, but it was the kind of thing that I had to see with my own eyes. I consulted YouTube to see if I could find footage of this match, and the online archive duly obliged me; I found an eight-minute highlight reel, dated 29 March 2009, in which Eastleigh, playing at home, had defeated AFC Wimbledon by 2–1. The crowd was in vibrant mood; the attendance was 2,283, a record for the club, reflecting both the fact that AFC Wimbledon were visiting and that Eastleigh were making an excellent challenge for the Blue Square Football Conference South championship, which carried with it the division's sole promotion place.

Traffic at the top of the league table was congested, to say the least. AFC Wimbledon had three games of the season to go, one of which was against the second-placed team, Hampton; Eastleigh were ten points behind Wimbledon, but had played two games fewer. Unsurprisingly, given these substantial stakes, the first half of the contest was goalless, Wimbledon lofting a series of high balls towards the Eastleigh penalty area like half-hearted warning shots. And then, three minutes into the highlight film and fifteen minutes into the second half, came the injustice of which Brown spoke.

Eastleigh had won a corner; the ball was looped in from the right, taking a slow, soporific flight towards the far post, when it was interrupted by Tom Jordan, the Eastleigh centre-back and captain, who thrust up his arm and, as if he were channelling the spirit of some beach volleyball star, spiked the ball into the net. The referee's failure to spot the infringement was impressive, considering that Jordan was probably the tallest man in the stadium, and with his arm fully extended he could almost threaten the floodlights for height.

Following the match, Eastleigh's response in the media was perhaps predictably gleeful. Tom Jordan, joyously unrepentant, said that the ball "brushed off my head, rolled down my shoulder and went in". The *Wimbledon Guardian*, meanwhile, carried the barely suppressed sniggers of David Malone, the Eastleigh director of football. "Even if it was a handball," said Malone, "the laws of football dictate that you dust yourself down and get on with it. Wimbledon are too used to having things their own way, and I think they would struggle at a higher level as they lack resiliency." What did Terry Brown think of all this? He almost groaned: "You can't believe the pain."

More pain, unfortunately, had followed for Terry Brown. The Eastleigh decision had only been the beginning of it. The next week, AFC Wimbledon would travel to Bromley, where a victory would see them take the championship. Wimbledon, or the Dons, acquitted themselves well, so much so that they were leading 2–1 at the end of normal time, with only a few seconds of stoppages to go. With Eastleigh having lost, with Hampton, their closest challengers, having drawn, promotion was only moments away. And yet, *and yet*.

With the referee considering just how long a peep he was going to take on his final whistle, one of Wimbledon's players fell injured in his own penalty area; one of his team-mates kicked the ball into touch so that he could recover. Now, normal footballing etiquette would dictate that the ball was kicked to the Wimbledon goalkeeper, so that he could restart play. However, from Bromley's throw-in, Ryan Hall flicked the ball up right on the left-hand touchline, some 45 yards out, and floated an exquisite lob – well, in truth a hopeful punt – over the Wimbledon goalkeeper's head, and in off the top of the right-hand post.

There was bedlam. On the touchline, Brown was a picture of helpless anguish and gnashing teeth. On the pitch, Wimbledon players were despondent as Bromley shrugged or chortled their way back to the restart; the home crowd howled their delight.

To paraphrase the American poet Amiri Baraka and his seminal piece "Something in the Way of Things", this match wasn't proof that the God of Football didn't exist; it was proof that the Devil of Football did. On the importance of luck, George Borg was as adamant as on any other issue that I'd raised with him. "Luck is a big factor in football," he said. "It doesn't matter how good you are, how well you set your team up, what system you play – it doesn't matter… when you set up a team, I believe, in my own opinion, you still need at least 50 per cent luck."

Fifty per cent? That seemed to me to be too high, but an illustrious Italian thought that Borg had got it pretty much spot on. In *The Prince*, Niccolò Machiavelli wrote an entire chapter on this topic, entitled "On the Extent to which Fortune wields power in the affairs of men, and on how this is to be resisted"; here, he more or less confirmed Borg's estimate. "Fortune," he wrote, "seems to be the arbiter of half of our actions, but she does leave us the other half, or almost the other half, in order that our free will may prevail."

Machiavelli seemed to think that, if you just tried hard enough, you could simply thrash Fate into submission. "In my view… it is better to be impetuous than cautious, because Fortune is a woman, and if you wish to dominate her you must beat her and batter her. It is clear that she will let herself be won by men who are impetuous rather than those who step cautiously."

If we sidestep Machiavelli's medieval, if not Neanderthal, approach to domestic relations, then he seems to be saying that fortune favours the brave. Well, that might have been true if sixteenth-century backstabbing was your line of business, as it was Machiavelli's, but it was still to be seen whether that approach would work for a team trying to escape the Blue Square Football Conference South. Terry Brown's AFC Wimbledon team had been plenty brave enough – they'd scored a dozen goals more than their nearest rivals over the course of the year – but it seemed as though their luck had deserted them, that they might even now be caught.

For their trouble – such were the joys thrown up by the fixture list – they were now to play away from home against Hampton & Richmond, who were second in the league, in front of several thousand hostile fans. Here they had to earn a point in order to be virtually sure of the championship. I could see why Brown was "burning up".

When it came down to it, I think that's why Helenio Herrera and other managers hated talking about luck. By definition, managers are control freaks; for the most part, they can't bear the thought that, even after all of their meticulous preparation, luck plays a role in the outcome of a match or championship. It almost makes a mockery of all the hard work that they've done.

But it's unavoidable. Luck doesn't just play a role, but an enormous one. And the best managers are those who not only accept this grudgingly, but embrace it; who understand that they're one agonising degree removed from the action, that once the match is underway they're largely as helpless as any of us in the stands. Accepting their own helplessness is something that, traditionally, managers don't do all that well, and so there's a certain kind of bravery in that.

There's rarely anything other than luck that will divide two brilliantly drilled teams, and the moment you throw caution to the wind, Fate has an uncanny way of filling your sails. When people look back over Sir Alex Ferguson's trophy collection, me included, they don't regard his UEFA European Champions League victories in 1999 and 2008 as diminished just because they were earned for the most part through chance. They don't sit there and think that in 1999 Manchester United's triumph was any less real, even though Bayern Munich were dominant for much of the 90 minutes, hit the woodwork twice and were then only sunk 2–1 by the late, late goalscoring substitutes of Teddy Sheringham and Ole Gunnar Solskjaer. In many ways, poorly though United played that night, this is the victory of theirs that most neutrals revere.

Neither do people generally sit there and think that, in 2008, it wasn't Manchester United who won the trophy but John Terry who lost it for Chelsea, slipping all ends up in the act of striking the ball during that penalty shoot-out. What they tend to think is: Ferguson has been European champion twice, which is less than Bob Paisley, but more than most men who anxiously toed the touchline. So it's not even as if the general public will hold it against you if you earn your baubles not through genius, but through freak or fluke. But, more to the point, did AFC Wimbledon's Terry Brown earn his bauble? After two straight weeks of woe, would the God of Football smile upon him, or smite him?

In the third consecutive match in which chance would play a decisive part, the balance finally fell Brown's way. Losing 1–0 away to Hampton with three minutes to go, about to fall behind in the race for the championship, AFC Wimbledon made an innocuous foray down Hampton's left flank; the home crowd rumbled in anticipation, perhaps preparing their voices for their victorious roar at the final whistle. But that's when something happened that would have made Helenio Herrera kiss his teeth. Two of Hampton's defenders, their right-back and centre-back, swung their legs wildly to clear the bouncing ball but ended up only hacking each other to the turf. Wimbledon, all thoughts of chivalry tossed aside, played on whilst the defenders writhed in pain, crossing the ball into the vacant area, where it found its way to the head of Jon Main, who'd scored 32 league goals already that season.

So 1–1 it was, and Brown went predictably wild. From the video, it's not clear why AFC Wimbledon's luck changed: maybe it had done so because Terry Brown had finally accepted that he was helpless thirteen minutes previously, and thrown on Jon Main in a desperate substitution as some kind of sacrifice to the God of Football. We'll never know.

DIPLOMACY

There are many theories as to the diverse roles that a great manager must play: indeed, the thoughts of the well-travelled Paul Jewell on this matter are set out in this book's introduction. Yet John Foot, in his *Calcio: A History of Italian Football*, has provided a character profile that's even more satisfying – and almost complete, save for one omission. Foot considers that "a top manager is expected to be a combination of soothsayer, psychologist, financial wizard, fortune teller, propagandist and press officer". That's all true: but the one other thing that a top manager must be is a diplomat.

Diplomacy is defined in the *New Penguin English Dictionary* as "skill and tact in handling affairs or dealing with people"; this definition barely does justice to the ability to keep millions of followers happy, which is the necessary lot of the managers of the world's biggest teams. It's difficult to find an appropriate metaphor within football to describe the pressure that managers face in this context; but, fortunately, we can use a Hollywood movie by way of illustration.

Now *Reign of Fire*, in which a terrifying legion of giant flying dragons takes over our planet, is actually a pretty good film. (I say this because Rotten Tomatoes, the respected review website, gave it an unfairly low rating of 40 per cent, with the dismissive words "an enjoyable B-movie if you don't use your brain".) Perhaps its most memorable moment comes when the heroes are attempting to catch one of these fire-breathing horrors; to do so, three hard-bitten soldiers, or "Archangels", are required to leap headlong out of helicopters so that the supersonic dragon can chase them into a large airborne net. This is a pretty thankless task, which inevitably ends with the soldiers being fried to a crisp. Aboard the helicopter Christian Bale, one of the heroes, is introduced to the Archangels, in front of whom it is announced that their average life expectancy, from taking their imminent jump, is seventeen seconds. Their facial expressions are a picture of timeless misery.

Avram the Archangel

Avram Grant, during his tenure at Chelsea in 2007–08, often had the facial expression of an Archangel; and rightly so, because his career was only slightly longer. That's unsurprising. He'd replaced – some would say, usurped – José Mourinho, perhaps the most popular manager in the club's history, and certainly the most successful. Between 2004 and 2007 Mourinho had claimed two Premier League titles, two Carling Cups and one FA Cup; most significantly, he'd brought Chelsea their first league championship in fifty years. Yet he'd apparently fallen out with Chelsea's owner, Roman Abramovich, over issues of team selection and transfer policy, and so he had to go.

Grant therefore stepped into the breach or, more appropriately, the abscess. Rarely has a diplomat had so many parties to appease at once, each of whose grievances were coming at him with the speed and incandescence of those flying dragons. First there were the fans, who were dismayed over Mourinho's departure; under José, they felt, they could permanently unseat Manchester United from the head of the Premier League's high table, but now they had a new manager about whom they knew nothing. Then there were the journalists, who had parallel axes to grind, one being that, like the fans, they didn't know who Grant was; the other, that during Mourinho's time in charge they'd never had it so good. Writing engrossing copy about the man who had called himself "The Special One" was almost as easy as turning up to a press conference and pressing the record button. So quotable was José Mourinho that, with the exception of Brian Clough, you'd have to turn to other sports altogether, to boxing and to Muhammad Ali, to find another man so skilled in the art of filling Dictaphones. But now, having been spoiled rotten by this patron saint of soundbites, they were faced with Grant, a man whose stern features suggested that he'd chew each syllable before letting it out into the world.

The players were also taken aback, to say the least. Some of them, most notably Frank Lampard and Didier Drogba, were reported to have been in tears upon Mourinho's sudden departure. There were rumours of resentment, fears that Grant had nothing like his predecessor's pedigree. There might also have been the odd agent hearing these dark tidings from his client, and mentally preparing him and his superstar charge for the poker processes of transfer or contract renegotiation.

And we haven't even addressed the sheer weight of silent heartbreak among the nation's women, given that Mourinho was as handsome as any of the leading men in *Reign of Fire*. Grant, whose jowl was perhaps craggily attractive in a Mount Rushmore sort of way, wouldn't set hearts so swiftly racing. So here Grant was: with a public who didn't fancy his team's football, with a press who didn't fancy his words, with a team who didn't fancy his resumé, and with an owner who didn't fancy failure. You wouldn't have blamed him if he'd confessed that there were times that his Chelsea days felt like a B-movie.

So, given all of that, how did Grant do? Superbly, by any objective account. His team reached the final of the Carling

Cup and the UEFA Champions League, losing both, but by the narrowest of margins, a goal in the former case and a penalty shoot-out in the latter. His team remained unbeaten at home during the entire Premier League season, and ended up with a points total of 85; only two fewer than Manchester United, who only secured the championship by defeating Wigan Athletic 2–0 away on the final day of the league campaign.

But it was clear, even as Chelsea chased Manchester United to the wire in both domestic and European tournaments, that Avram Grant would have been sacked pretty much whatever he did. UEFA's Andy Roxburgh, writing of his pitch-side demeanour that season in the *UEFA Champions League Technical Report 2007/08*, referred to Grant as "dignified" which is as close as he could diplomatically come to the phrase "dead man walking".

We can't be too teary-eyed about Grant's dismissal; a reputed compensation cheque of £5.2 million must have gone some way to softening his ambition's landing. What's more, Grant could have reflected that he was in excellent company. Jupp Heynckes and Vicente del Bosque had also been sacked by way of thanks for leading their teams to the final of the UEFA Champions League. They'd both been laid off by Real Madrid, in 1998 and 2002 respectively; what's more, they'd actually won the trophy. Though they'd succeeded on the field, they failed to keep the punters happy – in other words, to "play the game".

Pigs and other chairmen

Picking your way through the rancour and rivalries at a club like Real Madrid requires exceptional cunning. Between 1998 and 2008, they got through managers at the rate of one per year; one of them, José Antonio Camacho, lasted only six games in the dugout at Madrid's Santiago Bernabéu stadium. Another, the former Liverpool and Wales striker John Toshack, committed perhaps the most glorious managerial suicide in the history of football. Having publicly criticised the practices of the club president Lorenzo Sanz, Toshack was ordered to retract his words or face the sack. To which Toshack replied, with apparent relish: "You're more likely to see a pig flying over the Bernabéu." The Spanish press was delighted. Unable to find a direct translation for this idiom, they instead responded with a flurry of cartoons depicting the scene, the sight of which left Sanz so outraged that Toshack was soon – and somewhat triumphantly – dismissed.

In fact, you sometimes wonder if there's something in the water in Madrid; its football clubs seem to attract uniquely belligerent presidents. Madrid's other club, Atlético, was for many years dominated by its president, the property magnate Jesús Gil y Gil, who could have taught General Franco a thing or two about control freakery. Gil was, to put it mildly, a controversial figure; in 1969, he was sentenced to jail for five years when the collapse of a complex he had built led to the death of fifty-eight people. (Incidentally, it was Franco who reduced Gil's sentence to eighteen months.)

We can be fairly certain that Brian Glanville, the celebrated football writer, didn't like Gil, because the obituary he penned for him in the *Guardian* in 2004 was probably the closest thing to a late two-footed tackle that you'll ever see in literature. It didn't take Glanville long to get stuck in, describing the former mayor of Marbella only five lines in as "football's rogue elephant", and then asserting that he "ate managers for breakfast"; a claim not without substance, as Gil, during his tenure at Atlético between 1987 and 2003, dismissed no less than fourteen managers. Having set the tone, Glanville then laid bare the bones of this autocrat's regime:

Gil laid down draconian conditions for his coaches. 1. He had to agree his team choice with the president; 2. Gil was allowed access to the dressing-room before, during and after a game to give instructions; 3. Economic and financial came above technical-tactical considerations – so if a player held out on a contract, he should be "benched", ostracised and ideally replaced by a youngster; 4. All criticisms by the president must be accepted by the coach; 5. The coach must play private detective, following players around by night; 6. When the president was absent, the coach must follow the orders of the technical secretary (nicknamed 'the spy'); 7. The coach [must] play no part in transfer policy; 8. The president was to have absolute jurisdiction over players' fitness, whatever the coach and trainer might think.

As Glanville related, Gil's philosophy was a straightforward one. "'I'm the one who pays,' he once said, 'so I do what I like. The coach should train the players well, and explain their tactics on the blackboard. I'll do the rest.'"

Britain vs. the continent

Broadly speaking, there are two different types of basic power structure that govern football clubs. One of those is the type you find in Britain, and the other, referred to by its critics with a disdainful sniff as "Continental" is the type you find everywhere else.

The British system was pioneered, like so many other things, by Arsenal's Herbert Chapman in the 1930s, and has been adopted with enthusiasm down the years by luminaries such as Don Revie, Brian Clough and the ultimate inheritor of Chapman's mantle at Arsenal, Arsène Wenger. Simply put, its ethos is that of a one-party state; the manager is ultimately responsible for everything: for the coaching, the scouting, the buying and the selling of players. The British school of thought is that, if the manager is to be ultimately accountable for results on the football field, then he should be in control of all elements of the football process. By contrast, the Continental system is a similar set-up to that of, say, a FTSE-100 company, with a far more fragmented model of authority. In *Calcio*, Foot describes how things work in Italy:

Italian managers are... team players. In fact, they are not known as managers but as *tecnici* – technicians. Italian clubs have – in the modern era – been run by a triumvirate. First there is the president, who is usually also the man with the money, and is the real boss. Then comes the CT (Commissario Tecnico, for the national team only) or *tecnico*, who chooses the teams and, in theory, decides tactics. Finally we have the sporting director (DS) who does everything else. Unlike in the British game, managers do not decide on transfers. This power is held by the DS, who makes his decisions in consultation with the president/owner (who must bankroll all operations).

Here we see a clear division of roles; the owner and the sporting director decide which players to buy, and then the manager coaches the players to victory. It has a comforting rigidity about it and, if accepted by all parties, can work to excellent effect. One of the best examples of this is AC Milan, who from the late eighties until 2007 enjoyed sustained success with three great managers: Arrigo Sacchi, Fabio Capello and Carlo Ancelotti. Between them, they won Europe's premier club competition (the European Cup, later renamed the UEFA Champions League) on five occasions, in 1989, 1990, 1994, 2003 and 2007; they also walked away with the Serie A title (the Italian league championship) six times.

Often, however, the relationship between owner, manager and sporting director is an intricate dance, and, every now and then, people will step on each others' toes. In particular, a wealthy owner and a leading manager typically share many personality traits, and are therefore prone to spectacular fall-outs. The chief characteristic they have in common is that they're self-made men, who've struggled uphill in life against an avalanche of doubt, and, having reached the peak of their careers, they remain as obstinate or as ravenously insecure as they were when they first started their rise. That's all well and good, until the owner begins, as Abramovich allegedly did, to enter the manager's traditional territory.

Richard Bevan, the chief executive of the League Managers Association – effectively, a trade union for football managers – revealed as much in a May 2008 interview with *Sportsweek*, the BBC radio programme. Commenting on the Chelsea owner's increasing influence in this regard, Bevan related that he "was told that at a dinner in Russia, Roman Abramovich said that he wanted more involvement in the football side of the business. That is, and was, his true love. He said at the dinner that he had contributed '30 per cent' towards the club in regards to on-the-pitch activity – fairly unusual, from a chairman's perspective."

Fairly unusual: with that one phrase, Bevan showed himself to be the consummate diplomat, perhaps politely reminding chairmen that they should know their place when it comes to team preparation. After all, hiring a world-class manager and then second-guessing him on tactics is a little like hiring Michael Schumacher to drive a racing car for you and then informing him exactly when to slam the brakes on. Predictably, once Bevan had revealed this tantalising piece of information, the interviewer wasn't done with him. Which 30 per cent did Abramovich contribute, *Sportsweek* wanted to know. "Recommending and signing players," answered Bevan.

As Bevan would have known, there had been significant controversy over Chelsea's acquisition of Michael Ballack and Andriy Shevchenko. Ballack had arrived from Bayern Munich on a free transfer, his contract at the German club having expired; he had promptly signed a contract at Chelsea thought to be for £120,000 per week. Shevchenko, AC Milan's second-highest goalscorer of all time and a former European Footballer of the Year, arrived for a fee of £30 million, with a contract reputed to be £10,000 per week greater than that of Ballack. Both men looked past their best; both men had been acquired at the insistence of Abramovich, despite Mourinho's marked disapproval.

However, this wasn't so controversial – and not vastly different from the Continental model; the presidents of Barcelona and Real Madrid, as a matter of routine, signed high-profile players without their manager's say so. *Sportsweek* therefore pressed on. Had Abramovich, the interview wanted to know, interfered with the picking of the team?

Bevan replied that Abramovich hadn't so much interfered as engaged in "heavy communication" with his manager. "I think if you're one of the richest men in the world," explained Bevan, "and you've got a massive passion, and you want to drive Chelsea forward, you want to speak to the manager on a regular basis."

"Heavy communication", like "friendly fire", is one of those too-smooth euphemisms that instead of deflecting you from the area of scrutiny makes you stop and snoop that little bit closer. How heavily did Abramovich communicate with Mourinho? Did he email him copies of the Chelsea team sheet, with 30 per cent of the team already selected? (And which 30 per cent of the team did he pick?) Thank goodness that Mourinho's time at Chelsea largely preceded the rise of social networking sites, or else Abramovich might have been endlessly pestering him to add Andriy Shevchenko on Facebook, or spamming him with tactical suggestions on Twitter.

Hearts and Romanov: a boardroom with a view

George Burley knew a fair amount about "heavy communication" and interference by a club's owner. Burley, a Scot who began his managerial career at Ayr United and who would eventually go on to coach the national side, had an experience at Heart of Midlothian, one of Edinburgh's two clubs, that he'd probably rather forget. To find out more about this disastrous episode of club politics, I went and spoke to someone who'd witnessed it at close quarters, and who was, appropriately, a politician.

Lord Foulkes of Cumnock had been a fan of Hearts since childhood, and between April 2004 and October 2005 he'd served as its chairman; in this role, he'd been responsible for trying to find a rescuer for a club that had mired itself deep in debt. Things had got so bad that Hearts were facing the very real prospect of having to sell their ground, Tynecastle Stadium, to a property developer who sought to turn it into a block of flats. Redemption came in the form of Vladimir Romanov, who, like Roman Abramovich, was a Russian businessman about whom little was known, other than that he was extremely rich and looking to buy a football club. The game rarely frowns upon such newcomers, especially when they're as passionate about football as Romanov was.

"He was a football fanatic," Foulkes told me. "When I went into his hotel in Edinburgh and I had a meeting with him in this large suite of rooms, every television had soccer on it. I mean, he was really fanatical… He thought he knew a lot about football, about players, about tactics. In fact, like a lot of supporters, he thought he could be a better manager than the managers."

Romanov's reign began promisingly enough. "He was very friendly," recalls Foulkes. "There were good relations with him and although he was not the majority shareholder then, we were in the process of negotiating so that he would eventually become the majority shareholder." Romanov took a leading role from the very beginning; he was involved in the recruitment of two individuals of rare talent, namely the chief executive Phil Anderton, and the manager George Burley. Burley had been recommended by Sir Bobby Robson as someone of uncommon promise; like Robson, he'd managed at Ipswich to impressive effect, having earned them promotion to the Premier League and even qualification for the UEFA Cup.

Matters rapidly improved both on and off the field. Anderton used his marketing skills to great effect, securing lucrative sponsorship deals and overseeing a 100 per cent increase in season ticket holders. Meanwhile, Burley was steering Hearts to their best start to a season since 1914. As Foulkes noted, 1914 "is a symbolic season for Hearts, because we had a brilliant team then, and nearly all of them signed up for the army to form McCrae's Battalion and went out to fight in the First World War; and a lot of them were killed."

These men who'd perished in 1916 at the Battle of the Somme were tragic losses to their friends, their families and to football. The author Jack Alexander, who wrote a fitting tribute to their lives in *McCrae's Battalion*, told the *Scotsman* in 2005 that "I don't think there can be any doubt that it was the best team in Hearts' history. It was on the verge of becoming a side strong enough to win several championships."

McCrae's Battalion had found in Burley's team the most respectful heirs to their legacy: Hearts won the first eight matches of the league season, scoring twenty-one goals and defeating Glasgow Rangers in the process. Indeed, Romanov had announced his plans to shatter the "Old Firm" of Glasgow Rangers and Glasgow Celtic, the two-team oligarchy traditionally atop the Scottish Premier Division, and take Hearts for the first time into the UEFA Champions League. He'd been ridiculed then, but his predictions, now that Hearts led the division by elevens, weren't looking quite so fanciful. He'd been revelling in the ensuing attention; he "was getting all the credit. The crowd were singing 'Vladimir Romanov' to the tune of *La Donna è Mobile* and he was waving and wearing his scarf and on the television and radio and doing all sorts of things." All was well. Romanov had now become the majority shareholder, and the club held a private dinner to mark his formal takeover. But then, recalled Foulkes, "suddenly he changed. From Dr Jekyll, this nice, pleasant man suddenly seemed to become a Mr Hyde character."

"Romanov," continued Foulkes, "started challenging Burley on the team selection and having rows with him. He kept coming to me and trying to get me to do certain things. For example, he had a list of all the players and he would sit down with me after he'd sat down with Burley, and he'd go through each player and he'd say 'I gave him three out of ten, he was no good', and all this kind of thing. One [of the players] was Julian Brellier, the French player; Brellier was man of the match a number of times, but [Romanov] never liked him. There was almost this childlike interference, saying 'I know better than the manager'."

Unknown to Foulkes, Romanov had put together a strategy for Burley's removal, which, when executed, was as swift as it was ruthless. Having ensured that he now had the majority of board members on his side, he chose his moment. "We had a board meeting," said Foulkes, "at which Phil Anderton reported – casually – that someone had complained that George Burley had turned up at something smelling of drink. And suddenly young Romanov – Roman Romanov [the owner's son], who'd said hardly anything at board meetings before, challenged this and asked lots of questions."

Foulkes had done his own homework on Burley's work behind the scenes, and had been more than satisfied. "I'd been out to see Burley at training a couple of times, and I'd been out there to watch and he was always there, every morning, taking training; and I said to one of the guys, who'd been on the coaching staff for years, 'How do you find George Burley?' 'Brilliant, absolutely brilliant manager,' he said. 'He inspires the players, they love him.'

"But Roman went on and on and on; and, eventually, he moved that Burley be sacked. I moved against it, but we were beaten by four votes to three."

Burley was dismissed that same week, to be followed a week later by Anderton, of whom Foulkes believed that Romanov had become jealous. "When [Romanov] was talking with me about Anderton, he was unbelievable; he wouldn't even mention his name," said Foulkes. "He used to call him 'the wonderkid'." Foulkes himself lasted only a few more months, handing in his resignation in early 2005. Hearts, despite all this turmoil, finished second in the league, as had the lost generation of 1914.

Subsequent managers would fare no better under Romanov; Foulkes would hear from them that they would receive faxes from Kaunas, Lithuania's capital, with teams that they should play. Romanov would be watching the games on television, or listening carefully on the radio, keeping a beady eye or a cocked ear to proceedings. What's more, his meddling didn't stop there. "At one point," explained Foulkes, "it was suggested – never refuted – that he would make the substitutions from Kaunas by telephone."

Thankfully, Romanov became less interventionist as the years went by; perhaps he was slightly embarrassed at his earlier exuberance, or maybe he just found other things with which to occupy his time. In 2007, for example, he won *Dancing with the Stars*, a Lithuanian edition of *Strictly Come Dancing*, and then launched a bid for the country's presidency, which was stopped in its tracks by a probably relieved electoral commission who pointed out that he was Russian-born and therefore ineligible to stand. It's notable that his hands-off approach, which consisted of actually allowing Hungarian manager Czaba László to pick the team, coincided with the steady improvement, after a substantial dip, in Hearts' form.

All things considered, Foulkes was fairly forgiving of Romanov's early excesses at Hearts, putting them down to force of habit. "He's a rich oligarch," explained Foulkes, "and a former submarine commander; I just don't think he had known, or understood, the process of consensus and bringing people along with you. I suppose if you're a Soviet submarine captain," he mused, "no one can question your orders because lives would be at risk, you have to obey the commander and he would never have had his orders questioned." The uncharitable might say that Foulkes was so understanding because he was directly involved in the Lithuanian's recruitment; his ambivalence is probably due more to the fact that, had Romanov not intervened, then Hearts might have ceased to exist.

Offshore owners

Within the last decade, British football has seen the arrival of a variety of businessmen as owners of, or major shareholders in, Premier League football clubs. Their nationalities reflect the globalisation of contemporary wealth; Uzbekistan's Alisher Usmanov at Arsenal, Israel's Alexandre Gaydamak at Portsmouth. Some of them, like Chelsea's Abramovich or Manchester City's Sheikh Mansour, have come clothed in the robes of saviour, perhaps seeking to use their newly purchased clubs as the emblem of their empires.

All of these men sound like Brian Clough's nightmare vision. In his autobiography, as indeed in his career, Clough made plain his disregard for his paymasters. The only surprise is that he waits until page 105 to launch into his invective. However, when it comes, it's worth the dramatic delay.

Clough wrote:

I have never understood why men with such poor knowledge, or no knowledge at all, insist they know about the game in general and the needs of management in particular. The vast majority of them knew nothing in my days as a player, nothing in my time as a manager and the modern lot still know nothing today. Yet I continue to see them quoted in the newspapers and droning on in television interviews, trying to convince the public and themselves that they have the faintest idea of how football works. It makes my blood boil; it makes me want to put my foot through the television screen and I'd have done it long before now but I have a dodgy knee to look after.

Clough's bitterness on this matter had several roots, one of them particularly deep. Between 1967 and 1973, during his time at Derby County, he'd enjoyed perhaps the happiest period of his managerial career; it was certainly where he'd felt most at home. Arriving with Peter Taylor, he'd found Derby at the bottom of the second division, and through a series of brilliant acquisitions he'd won the second division title within two years and, remarkably, the first division title within three. It seemed no sooner had he and Taylor strolled into the Midlands club, that they were competing against the best clubs on the Continent. In the summer of 1973, they would reach the European Cup quarter-finals against Juventus, where they were narrowly beaten in a contest later found to have been adversely affected by the bribing of the referee: by the autumn of 1973, they were out.

The cause of their departure was simple; Clough and Taylor had fallen out with Derby's chairman, Sam Longson, and so they'd made a demand that either he went or they did. Longson stood firm, and so it was they, and not he, who would leave the Baseball Ground. Clough regarded this event as late as 2002, and possibly even up to his death two years later, as "the biggest professional mistake of my career".

At this point, it should be said that a notable characteristic of Clough's account of his life is its frequent and savage self-assessment. Hardly a handful of pages of *Cloughie: Walking on Water* go by without him berating himself, often fairly, for acts of foolishness forced upon him by his ego. Within its first chapter he's already told the reader that he's unintelligent ("when you're as thick as I am"), and drawn attention to his incessant vanity, referring to his "natural conceit" and to himself as "an arrogant braggart". Self-awareness – at least in retrospect – was ultimately not a problem of Clough's, and so even he had to concede that, at Derby, he and Taylor left "for childish reasons".

Clough did several things that presumably terrified Longson and most of his board of directors, including, on one occasion, signing a player – Colin Todd, from Sunderland – for the then huge sum of £175,000, and only deigning to notify Longson by telegram once he had done so. That's unthinkable at a Premier League club today, or indeed in any business with a modicum of effective corporate governance (something which, admittedly, the football world has not always embraced). Clough went about his duties with imperial aplomb, and was a constant and controversial presence in the papers, on the radio, and on television; he became a liability for Longson, whom in Clough's words "changed very quickly from the friendly, generous old man who regarded me as the son he never had… to a vulnerable individual who put his own interests, image and reputation before that of the club".

Looking over the events, even through Clough's eyes, that doesn't quite seem right. Longson's behaviour towards Clough was that of a man who had invited a tiger round to his house and then become alarmed when it inevitably became hostile. Even after Clough had left, there was a concerted campaign by players and fans and even one board member to reinstate him, and demonstrations for months afterwards. However, Longson – and, with him, the established footballing order – eventually survived.

The LMA

Had the League Managers Association (LMA), founded in 1992, existed back then, its chief executive Richard Bevan might well have found himself as a spokesman for, or at least a protector of, Clough's interests. (It would have been fascinating to see him try to get a word in edgeways.) The LMA's position, as the go-between when clubs and their managers were at loggerheads, often gave him a lawyerly caution when he expressed a view; it suited him to be guarded, and to let others read between the lines of his observations as they saw fit. Prior to joining the LMA, Bevan had headed the Professional Cricketers' Association, which was, similarly, a trade union for cricket players; his background in that sport was clear, since he played a perfect forward defence to any question.

Mindful of this, I asked him what he felt were the three main threats to a manager's authority at a football club. "The role of owners in the running of the club and their influence in football matters can present problems," he wrote, with habitual reserve. "The adoption of new management structures without a clear understanding of roles and responsibilities can lead to a lack of clarity in a manager's area of responsibility. And finally, the setting of unrealistic short-term expectations can be very destabilising for a manager… As the average tenure of a manager continues to fall, clearly the biggest threat facing a manager is time."

Of course, it's the owner that decides whether or not he gets that time; and he's getting more impatient all the while, with managers falling away faster than Arctic sea ice. In

February 2009, Henry Winter reported in the *Telegraph* that "last week's dismissals of [Chelsea's] Luiz Felipe Scolari and [Portsmouth's] Tony Adams means the average managerial tenure has now dipped from 3.12 years at the inception of the Premier League, 1992–93, to an all-time low of 1.47 years." Bevan was quoted in the same article, where he showed a flair for the soundbite. "We are 193 days from the start of the season and 33 managers have gone," he observed, "one every six days." Several of these casualties had come under the "new management structures" to which Bevan referred; in other words, the Continental system that Chelsea, Portsmouth and other clubs such as Tottenham Hotspur were attempting to impose on a largely unreceptive British footballing culture.

At Tottenham, for example, the replacement of Martin Jol with Juande Ramos in the 2007–08 season is often explained as a dark and dastardly coup, in which the popular Jol saw his power frittered away by Damien Comolli, the shadowy and unaccountable director of football, suggesting signings that he didn't want or need. Yet the dispassionate reality of the matter is that Spurs simply got impatient. Under Jol, they'd finished fifth in the Premier League for successive seasons, which was as well as they'd done for twenty-five years; they'd also come within a late Thierry Henry equaliser of qualifying for the UEFA Champions League.

That summer, Comolli and the chairman Daniel Levy went in search of a manager who they thought would establish them as part of the Premier League's elite, and so they aggressively – and publicly – headhunted Juande Ramos from Sevilla, whose attacking play had for two seasons entranced La Liga (the Spanish first division) and Europe. Jol, after months of knowing that he was on his way out, was thanklessly sacked; Spurs got their man, who they in turn sacked less than a season later, following an alarming sequence of poor results, signings and performances. A few months after his dismissal, the *Sunday Times* caught up with Jol in Germany, where he was thriving as the manager of Hamburg. Perhaps unexpectedly, Jol wasn't in gloating mood, but instead spoke in defence of the Continental system.

"It's a good structure," he told Jonathan Northcroft. "If you work with a football director who's your choice, or you're his choice, the system functions. When Frank [Arnesen, Comolli's predecessor] was at Spurs it was perfect. In business you do tests, interviews, assessments: football's the only industry where you hire someone, a player, only by looking at them. With a football director and coach at least there are two people sharing the knowledge. But if one coach leaves and the next one is changing ten or twelve players, what's the value of having the structure?"

In summary: systems don't get people the sack, other people do. Whether a manager likes it or not, he must to some extent wrestle his authority from the clutches of his chairman's ego, and there are high prices to pay when he pulls away too forcefully; however, there are also great rewards in store. Arsenal's Herbert Chapman found this when, in the 1930s, he fathered the British structure of football management by making a Magna Carta-style grab for power at Highbury.

The boot room and the Byzantine Empire

In *The Ball is Round*, David Goldblatt lists a series of visionary steps taken by Herbert Chapman. Yet among all these, writes Goldblatt, "The most profound innovation that Chapman introduced was to carve out a space of autonomous action for himself from the pre-existing structures of power in football clubs." As Goldblatt explains, "Previously directors had signed players and selected teams, the players themselves in their own informal hierarchies had organized the actual playing and trainers had provided minimalist training, medical and laundry services. The core of Chapman's new autonomy was his absolute control over team selection, team play and tactics."

On the face of it, this seemed a fair enough state of affairs. However, having looked at the British and Continental systems, I found myself with more sympathy for the latter. The main problem I saw with the British system was that it reminded me of the fallen kingdoms I studied for my A-level medieval history papers. These would generally fall when a long-serving ruler, typically idiosyncratic, accumulated so much authority and governed in such an esoteric fashion that when he or she died, his or her heir would have an impossible task. By contrast, the Continental system of management, with its careful share of responsibilities, allowed for a stately handover of power: appropriately, it was a Continental empire whose efficiency I remembered best from my sixth-form history studies.

The thousand-year Byzantine Empire, which dominated most of the European and some of the Asian landscape until its fall to Mehmed the Conqueror in 1453, was as effectively run as any administration in history. That's not to say that it was without its periods of internal chaos – following the death of Emperor Basil II in 1025, it had thirteen monarchs in just fifty-six years – but, in the main, its leaders didn't allow their various military successes abroad to blind them to questions of succession at home. Alexius I Comnenus, who came to power aged just twenty-four, could have given Vladimir Romanov a stern lecture on the virtues of long-term planning. Taking the throne in 1081, and seeing that his son and then his grandson were groomed for power, he ensured an unbroken line of leadership until the death of Manuel I Comnenus in 1180.

Now, no football club has managed quite such a period of stability and prosperity as the Byzantine Empire; but Liverpool FC, with its Boot Room, is probably the closest modern example. Ironically, this most British of clubs had a Continental model of succession. The Boot Room was just as its name suggested, a place at the Merseyside club where the coaching staff would convene and talk football, and from which a procession of brilliant managers would emerge, each of them versed in the club's tradition of prompt and precise passing football.

This school, informal in its setting but its graduates as learned in their discipline as anyone leaving Harvard or Yale, produced impressive results. Bill Shankly, Bob Paisley and Joe Fagan, each of them proud Boot Room alumni, managed the club for successive spells between 1959 and 1985; this twenty-six-year period yielded nine league championships, two FA Cups, two UEFA Cups, one League Cup and – in the space of just seven seasons between 1977 and 1984 – four European Cups. That remarkable record was due to the managers and players. But, according to Hereford United's Graham Turner, there was one important group of people who were too often forgotten.

"I think sometimes chairmen and directors don't always get the credit they deserve for seeing the bigger picture," Turner told me. "It might have been that Bill Shankly was such a larger-than-life figure that they felt the need to go and get somebody similar in makeup to him. But they didn't," he said, referring to the decision to appoint Bob Paisley, a successor from within the club, instead of casting the net far wider. "They knew what they were doing. When I was a kid growing up on Merseyside, nobody went to watch Liverpool play. They were in the old Second Division, Everton were the big team; but Bill Shankly resurrected them. They thought that, when he retired, 'How could anybody step into his shoes?' He was such a dominant, charismatic figure. Yet Bob Paisley did it with the aplomb of a politician."

He'd witnessed at close quarters the growth of Liverpool, catalysed by the Boot Room days, into a national institution. "I had the good fortune once to go down to the Boot Room; [they were] fantastic football people," remembered Turner. "The depth of the knowledge that they had about people, players, and teams was absolutely incredible. They were masters of the game, and it just rolled on, the Liverpool machine. They dominated everything."

Turner was all too aware of the traditional, and perhaps healthy, suspicion that managers had for their chairmen. Johan Cruyff, who coached Barcelona between 1989 and 1994, took this distrust to a darker (and, as usual, amusing) extreme when he muttered that "every chairman has a black book". Pausing theatrically so that his interviewers could ask him to enlarge on this point, he then obliged: "Everything's in there. The chairmen of clubs like Barcelona are special people. They're used to everyone doing what they say. In that little black book they write down all the things you do to them."

The Hereford United manager, given that he was also his club's chairman, didn't keep a black book of grudges against the gaffer – at least, I didn't ask him – but he did have a far better view of the chairman's role, if not a wholly sympathetic one. "I see chairmen differently now; I wonder what the criteria were in some of their managerial appointments. Some of them baffle me," he confessed. "I can't understand from chairmen the kind of way the clubs are run financially, the level of wages they pay out without, on the face of it, the resources to pay those wages: hence the reason clubs are getting in trouble now."

For all the native wit of managers such as Clough, there's really very little they can do when a club's ownership decides that it wants things run a certain way. In that sense, the gift of diplomacy is of limited use; greater value lies in trying to convince these self-made men, who've succeeded at everything thus far in life, that they've just bought into the one business at which it's virtually guaranteed that they will fail. Those who treat owning a club as a magnificent madness, and regard the club as a fitful yet brilliant child, are most likely to keep their managers away from the guillotine.

RESILIENCE

Rude, ruthless and xenophobic. This is a trio of allegations that, in some minds, have partially tarnished the legacy of Sir Alf Ramsey; but these might not have bothered Ramsey too much, given that he remains the only manager to have guided England to a World Cup triumph in 1966. Ramsey went unloved by a large part of the media for his frequently short and scornful press interviews; his omission of one of the public's favourite players was thought to be cruel; and his dismissal of Argentina, England's quarter-final opponents in 1966, as "animals" created friction among South American fans that lasted until the next tournament, four years later in Mexico. Yet these three aspects of his character were evidence of the colossal obstinacy that he would need in order to win this most craved of trophies.

Leo McKinstry, in *Sir Alf*, his warts-and-all yet warm-hearted biography of Ramsey, bemoaned this manager's diminished legacy: "Part of the failure to appreciate the greatness of Alf Ramsey has been the result of his severe public image." This was due in no small part, continued McKinstry, to "the creation of a host of enemies in the press. When times grew rough in the seventies, Alf was left with few allies to put his case. The same was true of his relations with football's administrators, whom he regarded as no more than irritants; to him they were like most journalists: tiresome amateurs who knew nothing about the tough realities of professional football."

Coaching the national side

Ramsey may have put umpteen noses out of joint, but maybe that's just what a successful England manager has to do. The position is a notoriously difficult one, even by the standards of this demanding profession; if a first-class career in football management can be likened to the Aintree racecourse, then the England job is its Becher's Brook: few can come to it and remain unscathed. Following the dismissal of Steve McClaren in November, after England's failure to qualify for the 2008 European Championships, Arsène Wenger was asked if he would like to step into the vacant role. Wenger politely declined, recommending instead that the FA should appoint an Englishman; when pressed on who exactly that might be, Wenger's response was typically poetic. "I don't know who," said Wenger. "There are not many candidates because it looks a bit like a crocodile that opens the mouth and says: 'Jump into that.' Once he's in there, he's eaten. And once you have eaten four, five says: 'No, maybe I don't jump in there.'"

Ramsey could have taken heart from the fact that he was not the only World Cup-winning coach to be shunned by many of his countrymen. Brazil's Mario Zagallo took the trophy home a total of four times, not only as a manager in 1970, but as a player in 1958 and 1962 and as an assistant in 1994. He also coached the national side to the final in 1998, where they lost 3–0 to France, the hosts. Yet even these achievements didn't make him immune to sustained opprobrium: "I accept criticism, but what hurts is mockery. In Germany, I was elected the best coach in the world. In Brazil, I'm ridiculed." Zagallo and Ramsey's resilience were called upon repeatedly, in the face of discontent with similar roots; both of them were faced by a media and a public who believed that they were playing unnecessarily dour if effective football, at the expense of star players.

Zagallo faced this problem in 1998 when he excluded Romarío from Brazil's World Cup squad on the basis that he was unfit. Whilst a pragmatic decision, and one to which Zagallo presumably came to with little pleasure – he'd played Romarío alongside Ronaldo in several warm-up games, to superb effect – Romarío became eternally bitter, following a tearful press conference with the later revelation that he'd placed a caricature of Zagallo on one of the toilet doors at Café do Gol, a bar that he owned in Rio.

Ramsey's 1966 World Cup campaign shows the virtue of stubbornness under fire. The position in which he found himself with Greaves, and in which Zagallo found himself with Romario, is as difficult as any for a manager to handle: when there's a star player who millions of fans want to see in the team, but whose inclusion would upset the side's overall dynamic. "A good example," wrote Rinus Michels in *Teambuilding*, "is Brian Roy when he played at Ajax. You have to, even if the general public has a hard time understanding, let such a player go. For the best interests of the team, you are sometimes forced to make unpopular decisions… This is to the regret of the fans and the media who do not comprehend it," he continued. "We should not blame other people for this. You need to have a well-trained tactical eye to recognize the balance within a team. A coach watches a match through different eyes than fans or the media. He registers the individual actions and reactions as an interdependent cohesiveness."

This was sanguine stuff from Michels, calmly accepting the manager's lot, but he was far from naive about the stakes at play. He noted that, in a dispute between a leading player and a manager, the player will "almost always" retain the support of the board, especially where results have been poor. Perhaps the most controversial omission of modern times – since the player in question was neither, like Romarío or Greaves, unfit or lacking in work ethic – was that of Raúl Gonzalez from Spain's Euro 2008 squad. Luis Aragonés, the Spanish coach, had chosen to exclude the Real Madrid legend; a brave move, since Raúl was returning to very good form, had netted 44 goals in 102 appearances for his country, and was the all-time leading scorer in the UEFA Champions League.

Aragonés never made his reasons entirely clear, but there's a suspicion that he'd seen something nasty in Raúl's woodshed, that the striker's domineering influence would be bad for morale. In November 2004, for example, the *Guardian*'s Sid Lowe wrote of the trouble that Michael Owen had in breaking into the first team after his transfer to Real Madrid, with his difficulty being due to the machinations of one player in particular. "Raúl sought to undermine him," explained Lowe. "The only player to hold regular meetings with Camacho, Raúl urged the coach to leave Owen out and, it seemed, refused to pass to him – Owen made runs but was not seen. There appeared to be intention in the myopia and Raúl has used the tactic before, as one previous big summer signing privately confirms."

Aragonés' solution was simple; he went ahead and picked a squad whose members were all happy passing to each other at all times, he placed full trust in his players, and a harmonious Spanish side won their first major tournament since 1964. And, whether or not his critics fell silent, they couldn't be heard above the din of incessant celebration.

Busby, balancing egos

Player power – be it exerted by Raúl, Romarío or that unbreakable clique in your Sunday League side's dressing room – is one of the most significant threats to a manager's precarious position, which is why particular credit is due to Sir Matt Busby. Much is made of the fact that, in the 1960s, he had, in Denis Law, Bobby Charlton and George Best, three European Footballers of the Year in the same team; not so much is made of the fact that the three endured relationships with each other that were much less than cordial. And they weren't the only ones on unpleasant terms at the club; the atmosphere in the dressing-room was often so frosty that they might as well have dubbed the place Cold Trafford. Leo McKinstry, in a question-and-answer session in the *Guardian* in 2002, provided his assessment of the situation:

> Bobby, Denis and George were never close, particularly in their later years. Denis thought Bobby was over-rated… George Best found Bobby dour and aloof, while Bobby hated Best's lack of professionalism. So bitter was the Best–Charlton feud in the early seventies that they would not even pass the ball to each other… Bill Foulkes and Maurice Setters… were widely seen as bullies. John Giles and David Herd could not stand each other. The striker, Albert Quixall, was despised, partly because of his obscene habit of defecating into other players' boots. Harry Gregg, the goalkeeper, was feared as a maniac; he once sank his teeth into Shay Brennan on the training ground.

Reading that account, I think I would least have liked to sit next to Albert Quixall in that changing-room. Mind you, there would also have been the opportunistic cannibalism of Harry Gregg to contend with. All in all, it took a man of some strength to guide a team of such divergent souls to the success that Busby did; with this cast, he won the league championship in 1965 and 1967, and – most famously – the European Cup in 1968, being the first English team to do so.

Indulging in some amateur psychology, it's arguable that Busby's experience of the Munich air disaster gave him the fortitude for his success in later years. In early 1958 Busby was in charge of one of the youngest and most exciting teams that Europe had seen; nicknamed "The Busby Babes", they'd won the previous two league championships and had advanced to the semi-finals of the European Cup, having defeated Red Star Belgrade 5–4 on aggregate. Flying back from Belgrade via Munich, their plane had crashed upon take-off, resulting in the death of twenty-three passengers, eight of whom were members of Manchester United's first team; the average age of those players was just over twenty-three-and-a-half years old.

The tragedy almost forced Busby – who was sufficiently close to death's door to be given the last rites not once, but twice – from the game altogether. It's therefore fair to say that neither the serial squabbling of Best, Law and Charlton, nor the vagaries of Albert Quixall would have troubled Busby for extended periods of time. All told, he would serve as manager of Manchester United for an almost continuous period of twenty-five years, beginning in 1945 and finally moving to the role of director in 1971. In that time he'd win five league championships, two FA Cups and (of course) that European Cup, leaving in the meantime a legacy so intimidating that it would take another hard-hewn Scotsman, Sir Alex Ferguson, to inherit his mantle.

However, footballing institutions like Busby, who was never sacked, are rare, if not an anachronism altogether. Managers of humbler talent and achievement – which is to say, most of them – will have been acquainted with the dole queue at least once in their careers. Bobby Campbell told me that "you're not a proper manager until you've been sacked twice"; which made him a proper manager, having received the chop when in charge of Fulham in 1981, and Chelsea in 1991. It's also been said that you're not a proper entrepreneur until you've been bankrupt at least once; in both professions, therefore, failure is a badge of honour, a rite of passage. But it's also a luxury. The reality is that, according to statistics provided by

Dr Sue Bridgewater at the University of Warwick, half of all first-time football managers, once they've left that job, will never manage again.

A brief history of scapegoats

It's essential, then, that you manage well; that you manage with will. You'll face assaults on your resolve from all quarters, from players on the wane or agents on the take, meddlesome directors or pugnacious columnists. And you don't have the option of choosing just how much pressure you wish to take on. There are several footballers who, over the years, have been accused of "playing within themselves"; of refusing to move to larger clubs where the challenges are greater. One player who was routinely accused of this was Matt Le Tissier, the former Southampton forward, who scored 209 goals in 443 matches and rejected offers from AC Milan, Tottenham Hotspur and Chelsea. Le Tissier's career was one of consistent brilliance – and no little application – but it was conducted very much on his terms, in a setting where he was given ample room and time to express himself. Unlike Le Tissier, however, managers generally don't have the option of "managing within themselves": this is because they've become the not-so-proud inheritors of one of civilisation's oldest roles, which is that of the scapegoat.

We first meet the scapegoat in the King James Bible, in the Old Testament Book of Leviticus. In the sixteenth chapter, as an act of atonement for the wrongdoing of his people, Aaron selects two goats; one of them he sacrifices to God, and the other – the scapegoat – he loads up with "all the iniquities of the children of Israel, and all their transgressions in all their sins", and then sends it off into the wilderness, "unto a land not inhabited". All things considered, the scapegoat got off lightly, unlike the eviscerated goat whose blood was sprinkled upon the altar and the mercy seat. However, even the scapegoat's was a pretty raw deal, given that it was probably only minding its own business until it got plucked from its field and anointed as a vessel of the Lord's displeasure. Well, just over a couple of thousand years later, in 2008, the scapegoat was still getting a reliably raw deal. No longer wandering in the wilderness, it had just taken a job at a Premier League club, and its name was Paul Ince.

Ince had arrived at Blackburn Rovers with a degree of expectation. That was partly because he'd had a well-decorated career as a player, in which he'd won two Premier League titles and FA Cups and a UEFA Cup-Winners Cup at Manchester United, played for Liverpool, West Ham United and Wolverhampton Wanderers, and represented England fifty-three times. But, more pertinently, Ince had shown genuine managerial promise. He'd completed the Applied Certificate in Football Management at Warwick University and, taking over at Macclesfield when they were at the bottom of League Two, had saved them from relegation. He'd then gone on to Milton Keynes Dons, where, in his first season, he'd won a double of the League Two championship and the Football League Trophy.

Ince's desire to manage at a higher level was clear, and in May 2008 he found himself in charge at Ewood Park; his predecessor, ex-Old Trafford colleague Mark Hughes, had departed to Manchester City, following a season in which he'd taken Blackburn to seventh place. It seemed an excellent position, but Ince wouldn't last until Christmas. He was dismissed on 16 December 2008, having been in charge for only 177 days, and having managed Blackburn to only three wins in seventeen Premier League games.

On the face of it, these were more than reasonable grounds for an abrupt dismissal, given that relegation was looming on the Ewood Park horizon. But there were good grounds for

Ince to feel that he'd been thrown, if unintentionally, to the wolves. No sooner had Ince walked in through the door than he passed David Bentley and Brad Friedel on the way out, to Tottenham Hotspur and Aston Villa respectively. In Bentley, he lost a player who had provided six goals and eleven assists in thirty-seven Premier League games; in Friedel, he lost a player who held the record for consecutive Premier League appearances, and who was one of the best goalkeepers in England, if not Europe.

Meanwhile, Blackburn's leading goalscorer, Roque Santa Cruz, was about to undergo a dramatic slump in form. The Paraguayan had once been one of the world's most expensive teenagers, acquired from Club Olimpia by Bayern Munich for over £6 million. He'd made good on that promise in his first season in the Premier League, with nineteen goals coming at a rate of just under one every two games. Now, though, in a season where he'd experience injury and the deprivation of Bentley's service from the right wing, Santa Cruz – his head perhaps also turned by interest from some of Europe's more prestigious clubs – would strike just four times in twenty games.

Blackburn duly foundered, and Ince's services were dispensed with; yet, when all was said and done, how bad a job did he actually do? The experience of his successor, Sam Allardyce, gives us some clues. Under Allardyce, who prior to his arrival had had nine years' experience of coaching in the top division, Blackburn ended the season with 41 points, seven clear of relegation. Ince had earned 13 points (three wins and four draws) by the time of his departure after seventeen games; which means that Allardyce earned 28 points in twenty-one matches in charge. Had Ince remained in charge for the entire season, then, assuming Blackburn's form had been constant, they would have ended up with 29 points, and would have been relegated in last position. Had Allardyce stayed in charge from the start of the season, then Blackburn would have ended up with 51 points, in eighth place in the league.

This, again, seems fairly damning of Ince's performance, the risk of promoting a novice too far too soon above his station. Much was also made at the time of the fact that Ince was the first black person to manage in the Premier League, and there were suspicions that a white manager would have been given a longer time in the Blackburn job. Indeed, the *Mirror*'s Oliver Holt wrote an article that wasn't a piece of continuous prose, but instead a series of eight questions, each of them pointing to old-fashioned prejudice as the answer. Two of these enquiries were particularly pertinent: "Why do you think it took 120 years for a top-flight club here to appoint a British black manager? Why do you think people are calling for Ince's head when he's barely been in charge for 120 days?"

Tougher being black?

The answer, as with racism in all walks of life, isn't so simple to unpack. Football is a game where nepotism is rife; where managers are often handed jobs on the basis of informal recommendations by people within the game. Racism may or may not play a regular part in that process of appointment, especially since, in all honesty, there haven't been too many white British managers covering themselves in distinction in the Premier League in recent years. (Incidentally, the last white British manager to win the league championship was at Blackburn; the Scotsman Kenny Dalglish, in 1995. The last Englishman to take the trophy was Howard Wilkinson with Leeds United, three years previously.)

You could argue that globalisation, rather than straightforward racism, is the main reason why black British managers aren't now getting a chance in the top flight. With the entire planet to pick from, including nations whose managers receive a far greater level of formal schooling in the profession than they do in the United Kingdom, it's arguable that skin colour is less of an issue than it's ever been.

But we can't sweep the R-word under the carpet too soon. Leroy Rosenior, who managed at Torquay between 2002 and 2006, told the *Telegraph* in March 2008 that "chairmen tend to go for people they know… Relationships are built on first reactions. Some chairmen may find it more difficult to relate to black people. I think it's subconscious and I've talked before about a glass ceiling for black managers." Rosenior's thoughts seem borne out by the figures. At the time of Ince's departure, there was only one other black manager among the ninety-two in the Football League, Keith Alexander of the League Two side, Macclesfield.

Having been appointed at Blackburn, then, Ince was in a position to dispel whatever negative stereotypes about black managers may have existed: the only way that he could have done so was by excelling. That he wasn't given time to do so, however, was due to results rather than racism; a board of directors, desperate to remain in the Premier League, took one long look at the potential financial freefall upon relegation, and that was what did it for Ince. It was only a shame that, having taken a risk on a manager of evident talent, they lacked the courage to continue to back him. Eventually, Ince would return to MK Dons, and following Keith Alexander's untimely death in 2010 would find himself the only black manager in English professional football.

Relegation

Relegation: several of the managers that I'd interviewed had experienced it, and the word was an unlovely mouthful to each of them. "With relegation, you feel you can't sleep at night," said Bobby Campbell, speaking about it as if it were a tropical disease. He'd gone down to the old Second Division with Chelsea in 1988; and, though he'd brought them back up the following season with a record points total, the unpleasant memories remained. "You feel – with all due respect – not like a leper, but you feel that everyone's looking at you, you're disgraced. And the fans let you know, too."

Graham Turner confessed to similar feelings; he described his relegation from the Football League with Hereford United in 1998 as "without a shadow of a doubt" the lowest point of his career. "We were relegated into the Conference on the last day of the season, when only one team went down; and the first time we went bottom of the division was quarter to five on the last day of the season," recalled Turner. "We played Brighton here, and one of us was going to survive, one of us was going to be relegated. Brighton needed a point, we needed to win. And it finished 1–1. I've never seen so many grown men crying. It was bad enough leaving Wolves; it wasn't very pleasant having the sack at Villa; but that was by far the worst feeling of all. It was one of the reasons I stayed on, I felt responsible; and we've done everything we can to put the club right." However, Turner had been taken aback, and touched, by the response of the Hereford fans. "I had a delegation of supporters come to see me saying, 'Don't throw the towel in now, will you stay?' And this," he told me – still slightly incredulous – "to the manager who's just supervised them being relegated."

At some point, every manager has wanted to cover his eyes when a table showing his team's league position is thrust under his nose. One Arctic night in mid-March 2009, I went to see two of them, looking across their dugouts at each other at the very bottom of the Football League. Braving the evening with the aid of a well-heated Capital Connect train – we must give credit where it's due – I'd travelled up to Kenilworth Road to see Luton against Grimsby in League Two, to see Mick Harford's team play host to Mike Newell's visitors.

I'd been to Luton just the once before, to attend a literature festival, and before that I'd encountered it on two other occasions. One of these was in the pages of a book describing it as the worst of all towns in the UK; the other was in the pages of the *Sunday Times*, where a headline had joyfully named Luton's university as the worst of all universities in the UK. And now, it seemed, Luton had the worst football team in the UK. That was a lot of worsts for a place to take, and so I went to see how resilient the town was in the face of all this.

Kenilworth Road was correctly cast as a symbol of Luton's supposedly low self-esteem. It's a very apologetic stadium, tightly shielded on three sides by walls of terraced houses, with the fourth side peering over into a busy road below. It's a good twenty minutes' walk from the train station, and a slow trudge uphill into the final fold of a cul-de-sac; but once you arrive there it's all warmth, waiting on your affection like a shyly excited friend. I spoke with several of the season ticket holders before the game, and it happily emerged that the team, like the uni and the town, had received an unfairly awful press.

Though they were bottom, Luton just weren't that bad; in fact, they were pretty good. Unfortunately, they'd effectively been relegated before the season had even started. They'd begun the 2008–09 campaign with a total of minus 30 points; the FA had deducted ten points because Luton's directors had paid money to agents through a holding company and not through the club, and a further 20 points because Luton had come out of administration without agreeing a Company Voluntary Arrangement. Worse still, these onerous point deductions weren't due to corruption; but, rather the simple and sustained incompetence of Luton's previous board. An appeal by the new owners, the LT2020 consortium, fell on deaf ears at the FA; there was more than a suspicion that Luton, a conveniently weak target, was being used to show that the authorities could be tough when they needed to be. The Kenilworth Road side could have taught the Book of Leviticus a thing or two about scapegoats.

This, then, was the predicament in which Luton manager Mick Harford found himself: at the helm of a club which, less than four years after standing fifth in the Championship, was now facing demotion from the Football League altogether. In the match programme for the Grimsby game, there was a copy of the League Two division table, where a thin orange line – along with white and black, one of Luton's three colours – showed the position that Luton would have occupied but for the points deduction. They would have been in fourteenth place, a point behind Aldershot, and with a superior goal difference by ten.

At the start of the season, Luton had been so far submerged that Harford must have half expected Jules Verne to turn up; but sometimes nothing makes you more valiant than a lost cause. Those who saw Mick Harford's programme notes for the Grimsby game might have found them almost disappointingly positive. Given Luton's league position, you might have reasonably anticipated something like a pallbearer's diary, a romantic lament to the glorious years long gone. But what you saw instead was an account of the season that made it seem as though Luton were pursuing promotion, not cruising to their doom.

"I'm sure," wrote Harford, "there are going to be some surprises between now and the end of the season, so we must be ready to pounce should any of our rivals slip up." He wrote of keeping the faith and working tirelessly and working hard and still having belief and spirit and of still having belief again. In Tibor Fischer's debut novel *Under the Frog*, which chronicles the exploits of a naked Hungarian basketball team in the 1950s, one of the characters, Gyuri's uncle, is said to "thrive on adversity like a slap-up meal". Had Gyuri's uncle been at Kenilworth Road that season, or even that evening against Grimsby, he'd have been proud to have seen Harford gorging himself silly.

The match against Grimsby had a compelling subplot. The opposing manager, Mike Newell, had been dismissed by the previous board after he had criticised them for insufficient investment in the club; moreover, Newell had made a claim for several hundred thousand pounds against Luton for unpaid wages, despite the fact that they were in administration. When Newell came onto the pitch, then, there was clearly no love lost. As he raised his arms to applaud the home supporters, he was greeted with a murmur of boos, and the crowd's sour disposition only became ever more bitter once his team took the lead, with a header from a disputed free-kick against the run of play, on the stroke of half-time. I'd rarely seen so many cruel clichés piling up on each other like this; but, in a manner that was symbolic of their season, Luton pulled a goal back early in the second half, and, improbably, a winning goal through their substitute Asa Hall on the brink of full-time.

That result would give them a hope of survival that would turn out to be false; the final league table would see them finish 11 points behind Chester, the other team to be relegated, and some 15 points from safety. Yet it had been an odd season for Luton; they'd gone down, but not out for the count. After all, in the same year they'd gone to Wembley and, in front of a crowd of 55,000, defeated Scunthorpe United 3–2 to win the Johnstone's Paint Trophy. The touch and movement of their forwards – in particular Tom Craddock, a loan signing from Middlesbrough – didn't look as if it would belong in the non-leagues, yet that's where it was going. It looked pretty surreal from where I was sitting, and so I'd gone to see what Mick Harford thought of it all. I caught up with him as he was making the first of a series of pre-season signings, in preparation for life in the Conference.

"It's the first time in football that the League's ever lied, in my opinion," said Harford. "We weren't a bottom-of-the-table team in terms of the football we played, or the way we try and play. A lot of people thought it would be easier if they'd just relegated us and let us start afresh. It was harder than I thought it would be… if you'd won one or two games, which we did on one or two occasions, and got on a bit of a run, you were still 20-odd points behind, or 17, or 15; it was very hard to take."

The hardest thing from a footballing perspective, said Harford, was that teams would play against Luton knowing that they were looking to win every single match in order to preserve their League status. Teams would then simply sit back, said Harford, wait for Luton to pour forwards, and hit them with a smartly-executed counter-attack. It made life more difficult when, due to their points deduction, they were obviously vulnerable to each side they came across; every game was a little like swimming past a shark with an open wound.

However, Luton's relegation didn't seem all that bad. It hadn't come with the trauma that was traditionally associated with such an event, given that it had been on the cards from the very beginning of the season. What's more, the club had the peculiar comfort that comes when you know that a situation can't get any worse, and was all the healthier for it. "This is the first time for a long, long time that the club has been stable; financially sound, debt-free," said Harford. "This time last year, the wage bill was just touching £5 million, now it's around £600,000." I nodded, impressed. Who was the whiz-kid accountant who'd slashed all those earnings, I wondered. "Me," he grinned.

A few months later, though, Harford too would be gone. Often voted by fans as Luton's greatest ever player, twice-capped by England, the challenges posed beyond the confines of the pitch proved beyond him. His dismissal had made me reflect again, and finally, on the question of why successful players so often failed to make successful managers; and I realised I was asking the wrong question. The question was how anyone, great footballer or otherwise, made a decent fist of it; the question was, in a sport whose fans were ever more awash with delirious expectation, what success even looked like any more. Harford's reign had included a dignified relegation, and that vibrant triumph over Scunthorpe at Wembley; all told, it wasn't the worst mark a man could have on his resumé.

Survival

Management seemed one part glory, nine parts survival; since most managers went through their careers without a sniff of silverware, the one thing that any of them could reliably be judged by was their ability to hang on. This therefore made longevity the most significant achievement of all, which is why I had been particularly pleased to secure an interview with one of the managerial greats.

With the exception of Sir Alex Ferguson, there was no manager in British football who'd been more resilient than Vic Akers. On the verge of retirement, Akers had been in charge of the Arsenal Ladies team for twenty-two years, over which period he'd amassed a haul of thirty-two trophies, including, in 2007, all three domestic trophies – Premier League, League Cup and FA Cup – and the UEFA Women's Cup. When we spoke in May 2009, he'd just completed what he'd considered to be his most difficult season, one in which, nonetheless, his team had just won the domestic treble. I'd travelled to

Derby to watch the final of the last of those competitions, to see Arsenal Ladies defeat Sunderland 2–1. Despite the close scoreline, Akers' team had been a class apart, their swift movement of foot, thought and ball such that it could have been put together by Arsène Wenger. Following the game, Akers had stood bashfully by as his players had given him the obligatory immersion in post-match champagne; his body language gave a hint as to how reticent he might be in an interview.

Though Arsenal Ladies was the house that Vic built, trying to get him to boast about his achievements was like trying to get my friend's cat to play throw-and-fetch. You could beg; you could plead on one knee; but it wasn't going to happen. I'd asked Akers where he'd stored the vast number of medals that he'd won over the years, vaguely hoping that he'd built an extension or something to house them, and he'd had to admit that there wasn't room to put everything on display. But there was only one set of mementoes that he'd mentioned by name. "The girls have given me twenty-odd years of photographs," he said, "and they've all signed them; it's a big framed resumé of the career and how we've gone throughout the years. Kelly Smith did a photo of the League Cup Final with a nice message and note prior to her leaving [to play professionally in the USA]... and all those things mean so much more to me personally, as I feel then that the girls have respected what I've tried to do for them."

Akers, who was also the kit man for Arsenal's first team, had set up the women's team at Arsenal in 1987; it was an unpaid position, and combining it with his day job meant that he would often work from 8 a.m. to 9 p.m., seven days a week. During his time in charge, there'd only been one year in which they hadn't taken home any silverware, and they'd once gone 108 games without defeat, a mark which made the record of the men's team, a mere forty-nine games, pale in comparison.

Yet, in many ways, Arsenal's success was the problem; they were an organisation whose infrastructure was almost unrivalled in the women's game, their rude health a sign of a more general decay. "We [at Arsenal] look over our shoulders," said Akers, "and don't see too many clubs coming in behind us with great support [like ours], and that's quite worrying... Someone from this club will probably just have to say, 'Enough's enough'. We've worked our socks off to keep [women's football] in media-friendly areas, at quite a cost... and we've seen it at other clubs; when Charlton got demoted, the first thing that they got rid of was the women's team."

What really made Akers animated wasn't talk of his club's dominance; it was the thought that women's football in the UK was entering a crucial phase, possibly one involving its decline. "I think the game is in danger of going the wrong route," he said, "and it really needs to have an influx of cash. Somewhere along the line, the authorities have got to make a decision: where do they want women's football to go? Are they really behind it? Or are they just playing lip service to it?"

Akers was right to be concerned; a week after I spoke to him the FA, having pledged that they would establish a women's summer league in 2010, then pulled out of that plan, deferring the league's launch until 2011. Citing a lack of funds as the reason for this postponement, the FA said in their defence that they had made a record investment in women's football that year; but the sum they'd given, some £4.5 million, was less than a Premier League club would pay for a second-rate centre-forward.

The women's game, though, was made of stern stuff; it had been at a crossroads like this before. In December 1921, for example, the Football Association banned women from playing at Football League grounds. "Complaints have been made as to football being played by women," they remarked gravely. "The council feel impelled to express their strong opinion that the game of football is quite unsuitable for females and ought not to be encouraged." Without wanting to sound conspiratorial – and failing – it's tempting to think that perhaps there were conservative figures in football who were beginning to feel threatened by the fast-rising popularity of the women's game. Looking at the Football Association's website, it notes that, on Boxing Day 1920 "the biggest ever crowd recorded for a women's game in England took place when 53,000 people watched Dick Kerr's Ladies beat their closest rivals, St Helen's Ladies, 4–0." The ban was imposed only a year later. It would take a world war and about half of a cold war for it to be lifted, in July 1971; presumably women had proved themselves tough enough, and thus sufficiently worthy of the turf, in the meantime.

Forty-odd years on, though, and thirty-two trophies later from Akers, their game had still failed to take a foothold in the mainstream. "We are still very much a chauvinistic country," sighed Akers, "not like the Scandinavians or the Germans. Here there's a resistance to women playing football." He felt that matters had improved – his tone was optimistic when talking about how they'd overcome several stereotypes – but there was still something surreal about talking to a manager who'd been so successful, yet was barely managing to keep his own sport alive. But having seen how often Akers and women's football had overcome the odds, you wouldn't have bet against them doing so once more. As Sir Alf Ramsey said to his England players at the end of normal time in the 1966 World Cup final, who'd led the Germans 2–1 only to concede an equaliser with just about the last kick of the contest: "You've beaten them once. Now go out and bloody beat them again."

Zola, managing

Across town, at the home of Akers' fellow Londoners, there was a manager who was similarly battle-weary. Gianfranco Zola was sitting in his office at Upton Park as our interview drew to a close, his thoughts turning, perhaps gratefully, towards the weekend. It was a minor marvel that I'd been able to speak with him at all, as he'd had to rearrange our meeting on three occasions, often just hours before: what with the transfer-market frustrations and the threats posed to his job by multimillion-pound debts and takeover bids, it made for a traffic-jam of a schedule. I remembered something one of his compatriots had told me about football management; Gianluca Vialli had said that the key to lasting and thriving in this profession was being able to unwind. With that in mind, I wondered aloud what coping mechanisms Zola had developed. "How do you actually relax?" I asked him.

"Can you ask me the next question?" he spluttered, shaking his head with mock indignation at my impudence. "Relaxation… that's something I don't know, I'll have to look it up in the dictionary." Well, there had to be some way of getting away from it all, I figured. How about yoga, did he do yoga? "Yes, I do yoga a lot, I love it." Now we were getting somewhere, I felt. What about the pressure, the pressure? Thirty-odd thousand fans every week, and the expectation. Big-money signings failing to spark. Crowd on your back, players in your ears, TV pundits firmly in your sights. "You don't have to think about that," he said patiently, "because if you think about that you're not going to do a good job. You have to focus on the solution, when the problem comes."

But. But, I wondered. There had to be some sort of, you know, mental state, or Zen thing, that managers at that level put themselves into so that they could get through the days, the weeks, the months. Otherwise they were just like us –

merely coping – hoping – managing. There had to be –

"Look," interjected Zola, "I would *love* to say that I've got the formula. But I haven't got it. I've been doing this job for one year and a half, I can't be presumptuous enough to say that I've got the solutions for all the problems... No," he said finally, "I'm trying my best."

Try his best he did, but at the end of the season Zola would leave West Ham, his performance having failed to satisfy the club's new owners. Under his leadership, West Ham's Premier League status was threatened, but ultimately remained intact; something which, indeed, can be said for Zola's own dignity. In the end, that's all that most managers can wish for.

SELECT BIBLIOGRAPHY

Bandler, Richard, Grinder, John *Frogs into Princes: Neuro Linguistic Programming*, Real People, 1979

Cacioppo John T., Patrick, William *Loneliness: Human Nature and the Need for Social Connection*, Tantor, 2008

Clough, Brian *Cloughie: Walking on Water – My Life*, Headline, 2005

Eriksson, Sven-Göran, Railo, Willi, Matson, Hakan *Sven-Göran Eriksson on Football*, Carlton, 2001

Ferguson, Alex (with Hugh McIlvanney) *Managing My Life: My Autobiography*, Hodder and Stoughton, 1999

Findlay, Thomas *Garan 1631 to Muirkirk 1950*, self-published, 1980

Foot, John *Calcio: A History of Italian Football*, Fourth Estate, 2006

Freitas, José Carlos *Luiz Felipe Scolari – The Man, The Manager*, Dewi Lewis, 2009

Gill, Karen *The Real Bill Shankly*, Trinity Mirror Sport Media, 2006

Gladwell, Malcolm *Blink: The Power of Thinking Without Thinking*, Penguin, 2006

Gladwell, Malcolm *The Tipping Point*, Abacus, 2001

Goldblatt, David *The Ball is Round: A Global History of Football*, Penguin, 2007

Hamilton, Duncan *Provided You Don't Kiss Me*, Harper Perennial, 2008

Higham, Alistair, Harwood, Chris and Cale, Andy *Momentum in Soccer: Controlling the Game*, Coachwise, 2005

Hoddle, Glenn, Davies, David *Glenn Hoddle: My 1998 World Cup Story*, Andre Deutsch, 1998

Huizinga, Johan *Homo ludens*, Beacon, 1971

Lewis, Michael *Moneyball: The Art of Winning an Unfair Game*, W. W. Norton & Co., 2004

Lloret, Paco *Rafa Benítez*, Dewi Lewis, 2005

McArdle, David *One Hundred Years of Servitude: Contractual Conflict in English Professional Football before Bosman*, [2000] 2 Web JCLI

McKinstry, Leo *Sir Alf: A Major Reappraisal of the Life and Times of England's Greatest Football Manager*, HarperSport, 2006

Machiavelli, Niccolò *The Prince*, Longman, 2004

Maslin, Bonnie *Picking Your Battles: Winning Strategies for Raising Well-Behaved Kids*, St. Martin's Griffin, 2004

Michels, Rinus *Teambuilding: The Road to Success*, Reedswain, 2003

Mourant, Andrew *Don Revie: Portrait of a Footballing Enigma*, Mainstream, 2003

Peace, David *The Damned United*, Faber and Faber, 2006

Rivoire, Xavier *Arsène Wenger: The Biography*, Aurum, 2008

Tzu, Sun *The Art of War* (translated by Samuel B. Griffith), Oxford University Press, 1963

Wilson, Jonathan *Inverting the Pyramid: A History of Football Tactics*, Orion, 2008

Worthington, David P *Bill Shankly – The Glenbuck Years*, Baird Institute, 1997

INDEX